Other books in the Cognitive Strategy Training Series
Editor: Michael J. Pressley, University of Maryland

Cognitive Strategy Instruction that
Really Improves Children's Academic Performance
Michael J. Pressley and others

Implementing Cognitive Strategy Instruction across the School
Irene Gaskins & Thorne Elliot, Benchmark School, Media, PA

Teaching Students Ways to Remember:
Strategies for Learning Mnemonically
Margo Mastropieri & Thomas Scruggs

Teaching Test Taking Skills:
Helping Children Show What They Know
Thomas Scruggs & Margo Mastropieri

Using Textbooks with Students who Can't Read Them:
A Guide for Teachers
Jean Ciborowski, Children's Hospital, Boston

Helping Young Writers Master the Craft:

Strategy Instruction and Self-Regulation in the Writing Process

by Karen R. Harris and Steve Graham

Brookline Books

Library of Congress Cataloging-in-Publication Data

Harris, Karen R.
    Helping young writers master the craft : strategy instruction and self regulation in the writing process / Karen R. Harris, Steven Graham.
    p.   cm.
    Includes bibliographical references and index.
    ISBN 0-914797-77-8
    1. Composition (Language arts)   2. English language—Composition and exercises—Study and teaching. I. Graham, Steven, 1950-
II. Title
LB1575.8.H36   1992
372.6'23—dc20   92-6075
                                                     CIP

Published by
Brookline Books
P.O. Box 1046, Cambridge, MA 02238-1046

To Leah,
who has been and will continue
to be both teacher and learner as we
develop strategies and self-regulation
abilites throughout our lives.

Table of Contents

Foreword

Donald Meichenbaum
University of Waterloo, Ontario

In her thoughtful book on teaching writing, Nancie Atwell cites Kurt Vonnegut's observations about the art of writing. Vonnegut, in his inimitable style, observes:

> ...novelists...have, on the average, about the same IQs as the cosmetic consultants at Bloomingdale's department store. Our power is patience. We have discovered that writing allows even a stupid person to seem halfway intelligent, if only that person will write the same thought over and over again, improving it a little each time. It is a lot like inflating a blimp with a bicycle pump. Anybody can do it. All it takes is time. (*Palm Sunday*, 1981, p.128. New York: Dell.)

The present volume by two leaders in the field of writing instruction provides a much needed description of how teachers can help their students use their time wisely. The ability to write is a skill, and like other skills, it requires knowledge, strategies, motivation, and practice with constructive feedback.

Writing is also filled with emotion. Inherent in the development of any skill are many failures and frustrations. How writers (whether novices or experts) cope with such failures and setbacks is critical to the writing process. Consider that Hemingway revised the conclusion to *A Farewell to Arms* thirty-nine times, as Atwell notes.

But our students are not Vonneguts or Hemingways. What can we do to help the beginning writer, the unmotivated student, the learning disabled student, or poor writer? The answer is to carefully read, apply, and implement the guidelines offered in this book. Both Harris and Graham, who have hands-on experience in teaching writing, have thoughtfully and creatively integrated the literatures on writing instruction, metacognition, affective development, and cognitive behavior modification. They provide a detailed, practical, "doable" descriptive set of teaching guidelines, exercises, and examples. The byword of their approach is *collaboration*, as teachers are encouraged to share the rationale for what is offered, highlight the relevance of what is being taught, model thinking, discuss generalization, engage in conference dialogue, foster cooperative learning, provide constructive feedback, and the like.

It has been estimated that American students spend at least 70% of their class time listening to teacher-to-student talk. As Goodlad

(1984) observes, we talking teachers "are not responding to students, in large part because students are not initiating anything" (p.229). The present volume highlights the need to provide students with ample time to initiate and share their ideas in the form of writing. Harris and Graham also provide teachers with specific suggestions and instructional strategies as to how they can help their students use their time wisely. Teachers can influence what their students say to themselves before, during, and after writing something. The students' internal dialogue cannot be left to chance. Teachers need to influence students' automatic thoughts and feelings, their strategies, and knowledge base. Harris and Graham tell us how to accomplish this task.

To paraphrase Vonnegut, teaching writing is like inflating a blimp with a bicycle pump. The field is indebted to Harris and Graham who have made this process easier and more effective.

References
Atwell, N. (1987). *In the middle: Writing, reading and learning with adolescents.*
        Portsmouth, New Hampshire: Boynton/Cook, Publishers.
Goodlad, J. (1984). *A place called school.* New York: McGraw-Hill.

Acknowledgements

We thank the students, teachers, and administrators of Charles, Harford, Montgomery, and Prince Georges Counties, Maryland, who have worked closely with us for over a decade on the composition and self-regulation strategies shared in this book. While we cannot list here everyone who has helped or influenced us, we would like to thank the following teachers who have helped us in the development and refinement of strategies and instructional procedures and who provide many of the illustrations in this book: Nancy Altman, Arlene Bennof, Julie Burgess, Lisa Case, Lorraine Cochran, Stefanie Crumrine, Barbara Danoff, Pat Darlack, Dawn Eddy, G. G. Evey, Richard Gorski, Sarah Gosset, Susan Gray, Tricia Grove, Jane Higdon, Leigh Kudlawiec, Celeste Law, Mary McManus, Linda Metheny, Vivian Nelson, Sam Oliver, Andrea Ortoski, Sue Packman, Marilyn Pearce, Melissa Sexton, Robin Stern-Hamby, Carol Strouse, Charlotte Welker-Gay, and Clare Yates. We also thank the teachers and the director at Friends Community School, College Park, MD.

We also thank our colleagues, particularly Charles A. MacArthur and Shirley S. Schwartz, and students at the University of Maryland for their support and contributions to the research program underlying this book. Partial funding for the preparation of this book was provided by a small grant from the Office of the Dean, College of Education, University of Maryland. Barbara Torbert and Robert Reid deserve a special thanks for their assistance in the production of this book.

We also appreciate the numerous writers who have inspired us as readers as well as our teachers and critics over the years who have helped us to continue mastering "the trick of it." The first author especially thanks Michael Lyons, the high school teacher most responsible for requiring and teaching her to write. He provides one of the classroom illustrations in Chapter 4. Finally, we thank our parents, Jeanne and Warren Harris, and Reva and Roland Graham, who were our first teachers and models of self-regulation and strategic performance.

While our research into strategy instruction, which began in the 1970's, has been informed and supported by the work of a large number of researchers and theorists from numerous disciplines, we particularly recognize the four sources which significantly influenced our work from the beginning.

First, the work of Donald Meichenbaum (often called the Father of CBM), and his book, *Cognitive-Behavior Modification: An Integrative Approach*, provided us with the initial foundation and impetus for our work. Over the years his work has continued to be a source of inspiration. The early work on the integration of cognitive and behavioral approaches by Michael J. Mahoney and Carl E. Thoresen was also critical to our early work.

Second, the work of Soviet theorists and researchers, particularly L. S. Vygotsky, A. R. Luria, and A. N. Sokolov, on the development of verbal self-regulation, the social origins of self-control, and the development of the human mind, strongly influenced our work, as did social constructivist theories of learning.

Third, the work of Donald D. Deshler, Jean B. Schumaker, and their colleagues at the University of Kansas Institute for Research in Learning Disabilities on the validation of acquisition steps for teaching strategies to students with severe learning problems has directly influenced our work. It is interesting to note that among the influences on their research is the work of Drs. Meichenbaum and Vygotsky.

Fourth, our approach has been strongly influenced by the work of Ann L. Brown, Joseph Campione, Annemarie Palinscar and their colleagues on development of self-control, metacognition, and the critical aspects of strategy instruction.

Introduction

We recently asked a child in the fourth-grade to pretend that he was the teacher and one of his students asked him, "What is good writing?" Without hesitating, he shot back:

> "I think good writing is basically using your mind — brainstorming, putting your ideas out on paper, drafting it, and editing it so you have it perfect. Doing it step by step until you get it right."

A fifth-grader gave us a similar response when we asked him, "What kinds of things do good writers do when they write?" He explained:

> "Well they take all of their brainstorming ideas and put them on a piece of paper and just write the rough draft. Then, they come back and find mistakes and think of some other ideas and do it over again."

Finally, a young lady in seventh-grade provided a very cogent explanation for why some children have trouble writing. She exclaimed, "Some kids just don't have the know-how."

This book is about helping young writers develop the "know-how." Developing know-how includes helping students develop specific strategies for planning, generating, organizing, and revising their text, as well as strategies for directing and regulating the process of writing. In this book, we describe what we have learned so far about teaching these two types of strategies. We cover validated writing strategies ranging from brainstorming to the use of peer response in revising, and examine how young writers can use such basic cognitive processes as goal-setting and self-monitoring to orchestrate the writing process. In addition, we present a distinctive method, self-regulated strategy development, for developing and teaching these two types of strategies. While teachers have found this teaching model, or variations of the model, to be effective with a wide range of students, it has proven to be especially useful for children with learning problems.

Similarly, the composition and self-regulation strategies we cover can be used by all students. While all students do not need instruction on all of the strategies presented here, most could profit from learning some of these procedures. For instance, teachers can help students with writing problems gain needed security in the composing process and replace ineffective approaches with more productive ones by teaching them many of the planning, generating, organizing, and revising strategies covered. These same students and other students who already have effective composition strategies may profit from learning how to apply the self-regulation strategies presented. Teachers can also help good writers extend their capabilities by helping them develop more sophisticated versions of the strategies examined.

It is important to emphasize that we do not recommend a prescribed sequence for teaching the composition and self-regulation strategies covered in this book. We also do not arrange the strategies from most to least critical. Instead, we believe that teachers should decide what strategies to use at what time and with whom.

Organization Of The Book

In the opening Chapter of *Helping Young Writers Master The Craft*, the rationale for why strategy instruction should be an integral part of the writing program is established. We begin by considering what strategies should be taught. This question is addressed by exploring what skilled writers do as they compose. Our analysis shows that skilled writers have a powerful repertoire of strategies for planning, generating, organizing, and revising text as well as specific strategies for regulating the writing process. We then consider how strategy instruction can help students become better writers, and the value of such instruction to the overall writing program.

In the second chapter, the instructional model we use to teach specific composition and self-regulation strategies is presented. First, effective procedures for helping students acquire and successfully manage composition strategies are described. The implementation and evaluation of these procedures are then illustrated with a real-life example.

Chapters Three and Four provide detailed descriptions of the specific composition and self-regulation strategies we have developed and taught to school-aged children. In Chapter Three, a family of writing strategies for planning, generating, organizing, and revising text is presented. The effectiveness of each strategy is illustrated with children's writing, and suggestions for how to modify and extend the strategies are offered. Chapter Four provides examples of how students can apply self-regulation strategies, including self-instructions, goal setting, self-assessment, self-recording, and self-reinforcement, to help them better direct and manage the writing process.

In Chapter Five, the instructional model presented in Chapter Two is expanded by examining what teachers need to consider when planning and implementing strategy instruction in writing. The goals of strategy instruction are to help students master more complex and effective writing strategies, further develop their capabilities to monitor and manage their writing, and foster more positive attitudes about writing and themselves as writers. Chapter Five provides a structure for accomplishing these goals through basic, but interrelated and recursive, planning stages. Specifically, student characteristics and specific aspects of the writing process or task that teachers need to consider when selecting and designing writing strategies and a corresponding teaching regime are discussed. Recommendations concerning the establishment of instructional goals and selecting instructional components follow.

Chapter Six provides a more indepth look at one of the components included in our instructional model, evaluation. Principles for evaluating the effectiveness of strategies and the procedures used to teach them are presented. In addition, specific suggestions and instruments for evaluating strategy effects are included in the Chapter and an Appendix at the end of the book.

The final chapter is entitled, "The Trick Of It." In this chapter, we examine the role of strategy instruction in the writing classroom and provide some "tips" on how to integrate strategy instruction into the writing period. It is our hope that taken together, these chapters will help teachers and students use composition and self-regulation strategies as they master the craft of writing.

CHAPTER ONE

Cognitive Strategy Instruction and Writing

Formal attention to strategy instruction in writing, like other educational areas, is relatively new. Many teachers are unfamiliar with the arguments for using strategies and for this approach. The basic assumption underlying the strategy instructional perspective is that many students can be taught more effective strategies than the ones they learn and apply informally on their own. In writing, strategy instruction helps students enrich and upgrade their skills as writers by teaching them new or different ways to formulate and structure their prose and ways to improve what they currently do.

WHAT STRATEGIES SHOULD BE TAUGHT IN WRITING?

During recent years, theorists and researchers have developed reasonably cogent descriptions of the mental processes skilled writers employ in writing: one of the most striking findings is that their writing is goal directed and their goals are organized hierarchically.

An Example

A classroom teacher we know was asked to write an article for a local newspaper about the difficulties that students with learning disabilities face in making the transition from elementary school to junior high school. She approached the task by first determining the specific aspects of the topic she wanted to cover as well as her general approach to the audience. Because her intended audience was parents, she decided to concentrate her writing efforts on identifying transition difficulties that could be influenced by the students' parents. Moreover, she decided that the voice she would use when writing the piece would not be that of a teacher, but one of a parent who had faced this same problem with her own child.

Once she identified her major goals, she went on to identify a variety of subgoals designed to facilitate reaching these goals. These included: identifying a list of transition problems by reviewing her own personal experiences as both a parent and a junior high school teacher; consulting with her own child and other students with learning disabilities who had made the transition; selecting and organizing only those ideas that were amenable to parental influence; and using the first-person, incorporating personal anecdotes, and avoiding professional jargon as she wrote. These goals and subgoals provided guidance as she wrote and revised her paper.

Even though the planning process was already off to a good start (goals and subgoals had been established), she still had to apply additional planning strategies for gathering information (brainstorming and interviewing) and arranging concepts (sifting and culling ideas). To turn her plans into written prose, she simultaneously attended to decisions about word choice, clarity,and possible reactions of the reader while executing such basic text production skills as handwriting and spelling. Throughout, she was looking for ways to sharpen her ideas and her communication. She revised several of her goals and often found something better to say or a better way to say it.

This teacher clearly had a powerful repertoire of strategies to draw upon as she wrote and was able to bring these strategies and other skills into play when they were needed. Her example helps to highlight what students need to master to become effective writers. This includes strategies *for planning, producing, and revising text, as well as strategies for monitoring and regulating the use of these strategies and the overall writing process.*

Do Schools Already Teach These Strategies?

Schools generally emphasize helping students develop competency in mainly one of these processes—text production. A considerable amount of time and energy is spent teaching children handwriting, spelling, and sentence construction, and some of this instruction is of dubious value. For example, many of the language arts textbooks commonly used in American schools rely heavily on sentence transcription activities like copying a sentence and supplying the correct verb tense or correcting capitalization and punctuation. Despite their popularity, activities that concentrate on grammar, punctuation, or usage are not embedded in actual writing experiences and do not improve students' writing.

Production skills are not important. Failure to develop adequate proficiency and fluency in producing text when the goal is to communicate one's thoughts and ideas to others impedes students' writing development. School curricula need to give more attention, however, to helping students develop effective strategies for planning and revising text and for self-regulating their writing. These strategic skills are the foundation of effective writing.

WHY TEACH PLANNING AND REVISING STRATEGIES?

Teaching strategies for planning and revising helps students in two important ways. First, they become more secure and confident when they can use these processes in their writing. Second, as their confidence increases, their approach to planning and revising becomes more mature. They further develop and embellish these processes and make them their own.

Strategy instruction provides the young writer with several different levels of support. Perhaps most important, strategies provide procedures—called heuristics—a student can use to accomplish a particular goal. They help the student organize and sequence actions for attaining a goal. These organizing procedures enhance a student's performance, especially if the current approach to the task is ineffective or inefficient.

For example, a simple planning strategy such as having a student answer and make notes about a series of questions (Who? What? When? Where? How? and Why?) regarding an event, before describing it in writing, helps the student think about the writing task in an orderly fashion and makes the task of composing easier in several important ways. The questions help direct the student's attention to the most important aspects of the event to be described, and increase the likelihood that the description will be reasonably complete. The written notes provide a visible record of the student's thoughts, making it easier to add, delete, and organize ideas.

A second form of support involves the instructional components used to teach the writing strategy. Teachers commonly use a variety of instructional procedures such as *modeling* and *guided practice* to help students develop the skills needed for carrying out a new writing strategy. This support provides a bridge between the child's current approach to planning or revising and the flexible and independent use of new or more mature strategies. Instruction helps students learn to competently apply planning and revising strategies which they previously could use only with the help of a more competent writer.

Third, the instructional model presented in this book provides students with specific tools for regulating the flexible use of the planning and revising strategies (see Chapters 2 and 5). These self-regulation strategies include: encouraging students to set goals for learning and using the strategy and for their writing; asking them to monitor and record when the strategy is used and the success of its application; and helping them develop an internal dialogue for directing and evaluating their use of the strategy. The use of self-regulating strategies in tandem with appropriate writing strategies helps students develop more complex planning and revising behaviors.

WHY TEACH STRATEGIES FOR REGULATING THE WRITING PROCESS?

We believe all students should be taught procedures for becoming self-regulated learners — students who engage in various procedures to manage achieving their goals.

Self-regulation strategies can be viewed in several ways. First, they are *general strategies* that can be applied to a variety of academic tasks and situations. For instance, when trying to lose weight, many people set goals for how much they wish to lose, monitor their progress by weighing themselves on the scale each day, and reinforce themselves with a pat on the back or more tangible rewards if the desired weight is lost.

Second, self-regulation strategies when combined with other strategies, enable one to develop and execute a plan of action for accomplishing a desired task *independently*. When studying for an end-of-the-week history test, for example, a student might combine the self-regulation skill of self-assessment (periodically see if the answers to the study questions are known) with such other strategies as relating the material in the chapter to what is already known and paying attention to words italicized in text.

A third way of looking at self-regulation strategies is that they contribute to students' cognitive development. Self-regulatory procedures, such as goal setting, self-instructions, and self-assessment, provide information that students can use to alter what they do and how they approach tasks. If a selected goal is not being achieved, a student may decide on another course of action, and so set a new or modified set of guidelines for proceeding.

While we believe that developing students' self-regulation skills should be a priority in all academic disciplines, there are three reasons why this is advisable in the area of writing. First, they allow students to become more independent during writing. This has the added benefit of reducing demands on teacher time. Second, teaching students to use self-regulation strategies can increase their level of motivation and engagement with writing. Third, they provide students with the tools they need to orchestrate the composing process— a process with which many students have difficulty.

HOW DOES STRATEGY AND SELF-REGULATION INSTRUCTION BENEFIT THE WRITING PROGRAM?

Strategy instruction and self-regulation instruction fit well with the process approach to writing. In the process approach, teachers create an environment where students have time not only to write, but to think and reflect upon what they are writing about. Instruction takes place in a supportive environment where students are encouraged to listen to the writing of others, ask questions about their writing and others' writing, watch and think with others as they write, and share their writing with their peers and teacher. Students are also encouraged to choose their own topics, help each other, and take risks.

In the process approach teachers also support students by structuring the writing period, emphasizing the cognitive processes underlying writing, offering mini-lessons on subjects ranging from topic selection to writing procedures, and conferencing regularly with students before, during, and after they write. The process approach emphasizes student self-direction and sustained writing, allowing time for planning, drafting, and revising.

Strategy instruction and self-regulation instruction can be used to promote similar abilities. Teachers using a process approach often model or emphasize strategies for planning, revising, and directing the writing process during mini-lessons or teacher-student conferences. For instance, a teacher might model how to use a brainstorming strategy during a mini-lesson, or recommend that a student consider setting a particular goal for her paper during an initial writing conference.

While this may be all the support that some students need to help them come to own such strategies, this is not the case for many students, especially students with writing problems. For these students, the development of more mature writing processes often requires more intensive instruction and greater support. The explicit teaching methods used in writing strategy instruction are necessary to help these students develop sophisticated use of the strategies that underlie good writing.

Strategy instruction and self-regulation instruction also complement and support the social conditions that process-approach teachers strive to create. For example, teaching students to use a peer-editing strategy provides an excellent means not only for improving revising skills, but promoting collaboration as well. Students are encouraged to listen, share, ask questions, and help each other as they rework their papers. Activities of this nature help to create a social climate conducive to writing development.

Computers have been widely endorsed by educators as a means for improving students' writing. While the motivating and editing power of word processors offers considerable advantages, word processing by itself does not have much effect on the writing of many students, especially poor writers. For example, a commonly celebrated feature of word processing is the flexibility it provides in the editing and revising of text. Material can easily be moved, added, deleted, or typed-over — major advantages over writing with a paper and pencil. But a word processor is not a replacement for the writer's skill in evaluating what she has written, detecting problems, and making changes that improve the paper. For students whose basic approach to revising is to correct mechanical errors and make simple word changes, the full capability of the word processor will be wasted without instruction aimed at developing revising strategies. Strategy instruction provides a means for doing just that.

Finally, strategy instruction and self-regulation instruction should take place within the context of the regular curriculum, helping to foster attainment of broader school goals. Strategies chosen to mesh with the existing curriculum provide students with useful tools for handling daily instructional demands, and enable students with learning problems to learn within the context of the regular curriculum — a highly desirable goal.

Students need to realize that writing and self-regulation strategies should be used whenever one composes. When strategy and self-regulation instruction takes place outside of the context of the writing program or the school's existing curriculum, students are much less likely to see the relevance of the learned strategies to their assignments in school.

Similarly, writing strategy and self-regulation instruction should not supplant a student's writing program. While strategies for managing the writing process and planning and revising text are essential to writing development, they are not the only skills that young writers need to develop.

IS STRATEGY AND SELF-REGULATION INSTRUCTION RESPONSIVE TO STUDENTS' WRITING NEEDS?

The problems faced by young writers, especially students with learning problems, reminds us of Charlie Brown's dog, Snoopy. Generating content always seems to be a problem for Snoopy; his story line inevitably revolves around the opening sentence, "It was a dark and stormy night." He generally has no idea of where his story is headed, and his ideas for what will come next are produced as they come to mind—usually in reaction to a comment by one of the other characters in the comic strip or in response to what has just been written. And don't speak to Snoopy of revising. When Lucy or another character suggests that he change in some way what he has written, the change will inevitably be a simple substitution or addition. As with Snoopy, many young writers, both those who are achieving normally and those with learning problems, have difficulties with the mental operations underlying effective writing.

Generating Content

Many students have difficulty finding enough to say and usually cannot imagine discarding anything that might fit. For students with learning difficulties this problem is even more pronounced. Their compositions are often half as long as those of their normally achieving peers. One reason may be that we ask them to write about subjects they do not know enough about, rather than asking them to select their own writing topics. But many students also have difficulty gaining access to what they do know. Strategies for obtaining new information and accessing current knowledge, therefore, would be helpful to most students.

Planning

While planning among expert writers is generally goal directed, goals do not appear to drive the planning process for most students. Students spend little time planning in advance of writing (often less than a minute). Their planning during writing can best be described as "knowledge telling": simply writing down whatever one knows. Ideas are produced as they come to mind, with each preceding word or sentence stimulating the development of the succeeding text.

Students with learning problems approach the writing task in a similar way. As evidenced by the poorer quality of their papers, however, they are less effective with this approach. For instance, when we asked students to write an essay on whether it is advisable for kids to go to school during the summer, students with learning problems tended simply to give a "yes" or "no" answer, briefly stating whatever reason(s) came to mind, and abruptly terminating their paper. The whole process often took no longer than five minutes.

A planning strategy of this nature is insensitive to the needs of the reader, the organization of the text, and the constraints of the topic. Most students can benefit from being taught effective planning and self-regulation strategies.

Revising

The approach of most students to revising (even college students!) can best be described as proofreading. Few changes are made that actually affect the meaning or the content of what is written. Students with learning problems also focus their revising efforts on correcting errors of mechanics and substituting one word for another. This tactic, once again, is even less successful for these students. Their attempts at correcting the mechanical errors in their papers are frequently unsuccessful.

In short, the majority of students appear to use a "least effort" strategy when revising. They change what is easiest to change. Rarely do they restructure or rearrange their language once it has assumed written form. Learning revising strategies can meaningfully improve students' development as writers.

A RECAP: WHY STRATEGY INSTRUCTION AND SELF-REGULATION INSTRUCTION IS A GOOD IDEA

Teaching students to become effective and mature writers is a challenging job. A considerable gap exists between what skilled writers are capable of and what school-aged children can do. One of the major differences between these two groups of writers involves the kinds of composing strategies they have available and their ability to manage these strategies.

Clearly, the cognitive nature of writing must be attended to more directly in school instruction if students are to become competent writers. Strategy and self-regulation instruction provides a potent means for helping students obtain such competence. By teaching appropriate strategies for planning and revising text and for managing the writing process, teachers can help students develop increased confidence and competence in the processes central to effective writing.

While making cognitive processes such as planning, writing management, and revising strategies a habitual part of how students compose is a key goal in writing instruction, teachers need to do much more. Students need guidance and support to help them continually develop their use of these processes. Strategies cannot simply be taught once and then forgotten. Strategies will need to be upgraded and students may well need continuing support as they apply their newly learned skills across the curriculum. Good strategy and self-regulation instruction, therefore, is not a "one shot deal." Instead, strategy teachers provide students with ongoing help in developing more mature and sophisticated strategies for composing.

Another benefit of strategy and self-regulation instruction is that it increases students' knowledge about writing and the writing process. For instance, when teachers provide instruction on a strategy for story writing, students acquire at least three types of knowledge: knowledge of the basic elements typically included in stories, better understanding of what constitutes a well-written story, and understanding of how to regulate the writing process as they apply the strategy.

In summary, when strategy instruction and self-regulation instruction become part of the process of writing and writing instruction, there are several advantages for students and teachers:

1. Students are empowered as they develop strong tools for writing.

2. As students master these tools, they personalize them — make them their own! Students learn both how to use strategies in new ways and how to evolve strategies of their own.

3. Students develop knowledge about the use and purposes of strategies as they come to understand the strengths and limitations of individual strategies and how they can be modified and used across tasks and settings.

4. Strategy and self-regulation instruction assists students in developing knowledge about themselves as writers.

5. Becoming a more strategic writer can help students get the most out of word processing or instructional programs such as the process approach to writing by providing them with more effec-

tive and efficient tools for writing.

6. Teaching strategies that involve peer collaboration contributes to the development of a social atmosphere in which students work together—sharing, critiquing, and helping one another.

7. Students can be taught strategies that help them with the papers they write during the composition period, and their written assignments for other classes such as history, health, science, and so on.

8. Students are assisted in the development of more positive attitudes toward writing and themselves as writers. Thus, their level of motivation and engagement in the writing process increases.

CHAPTER TWO

Self-Regulated Strategy Development: Stages of Instruction

In this chapter we present our model for teaching composition strategies. Our self-regulated strategy development approach requires teachers to play an active, facilitative role in the development of writing abilities, through activities such as conferencing, modeling, prompting, and dialoguing. Teachers must understand the writing process and be able to provide students with direction and support as they develop as writers. They need to provide the level of structured guidance appropriate to each student, gradually decreasing this support as students master the craft of writing.

Thus, the same strategies are not taught to all students, and some students will need little strategy instruction. A simple procedure, such as explaining or modeling a writing strategy, or initiating a self-regulation strategy, may be sufficient when the student writes reasonably easily and communicates clearly. As the writer's goals become more involved or the student's difficulties more significant, strategy instruction as addressed in this chapter becomes appropriate.

The major goals of our self-regulated strategy development approach are threefold:

1. to assist students in mastering the higher level cognitive processes involved in the planning, production, revising, and editing of written language;

2. to help students further develop the capability to monitor and manage their own writing;

3. to aid students in the development of positive attitudes about writing and themselves as writers.

For students who have experienced a great deal of frustration, failure, or anxiety regarding writing, we find that the first two goals cannot be met without close regard to the third. The combination of understanding, control, structure and support offered in our approach has been very helpful to students, as have the sucessful experiences that strategy mastery facilitates. We have found a great deal of truth in the old adage, "nothing succeeds like success."

To help students master writing strategies and use them effectively, our approach includes the development of:

(a) skillful use of an effective strategy(s)

(b) self-regulation of strategic performance and knowledge of one's own cognitive processes and other learning characteristics (also referred to as metacognition),

(c) understanding of the meaning, significance, potential, and limitations of the strategy(s) (also called metastrategy information).

Our research and the work of others indicate that self- regulation of strategic performance and metastrategy information is important in helping students understand how and when to apply a strategy; independently produce, evaluate, and modify a strategy effectively; recognize meaningful improvement in skills, processes, and products; gain new insights regarding strategies and their own strategic performance; improve their expectations about themselves as writers; and maintain and generalize strategic performance.

STAGES OF INSTRUCTION

In the self-regulated strategy development approach, seven basic stages of instruction are used to introduce and integrate the strategy and self-regulation components. Throughout these stages, teachers and students collaborate on the acquisition, implementation, evaluation, and modification of strategies. We have used these acquisition and management procedures not only to assist students in the area of composition, but also to help students develop reading comprehension, mathematical problem solving, homework completion, and academic self-management strategies.

These stages are not meant to be followed in a "cookbook" fashion. Rather, they provide and illustrate a general format and guidelines. The instructional stages are meant to be recursive — teachers may return to any stage at any time. The stages may be reordered, combined, or modified as desired, as can be seen in Figure 1. After presenting these stages, we discuss six important characteristics of effective strategy instruction. Finally, we provide an illustration of one teacher's use of these procedures to help students master the story grammar strategy.

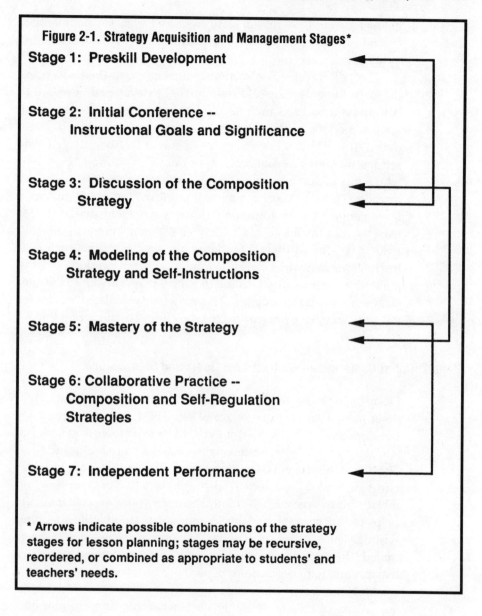

Figure 2-1. Strategy Acquisition and Management Stages*

Stage 1: Preskill Development

Stage 2: Initial Conference --
          Instructional Goals and Significance

Stage 3: Discussion of the Composition
          Strategy

Stage 4: Modeling of the Composition
          Strategy and Self-Instructions

Stage 5: Mastery of the Strategy

Stage 6: Collaborative Practice --
         Composition and Self-Regulation
         Strategies

Stage 7: Independent Performance

* Arrows indicate possible combinations of the strategy
stages for lesson planning; stages may be recursive,
reordered, or combined as appropriate to students' and
teachers' needs.

Stage 1: Preskill Development

During this stage, any preskills (such as vocabulary, concepts, and so on) not yet present but necessary for learning and using the composition or self-regulation strategies are developed. Preskills should be developed to a level of mastery adequate for progression into the next stages, but 100% mastery is not required; their development can continue into stages 2 and 3. It is usually best if preskills are mastered by stage 4, however.

Preskill development activities depend upon the learner and the skills to be developed. Preskills can be developed in regard to both the composition and self-regulation strategies to be mastered. For instance, the concept and use of self-instructions might be introduced here. The teacher and students might collaboratively create self-instructions relevant to composition. For example, a student who tends to act impulsively might decide to say to himself: "Remember, I need to take my time and go slow." Or, a student with a low tolerance for frustration might use a statement similar to that used by our Little Professor in Chapter 4, "I'm not going to get mad, mad makes me do bad." Students can practice using such self-instructions in a variety of situations as a part of preskill development; these self-instructions can then be incorporated into the later stages of strategy instruction. This may be particularly helpful for students who have not learned to use self- instructions previously.

Stage 2: Initial Conference—Instructional Goals and Significance

During this stage, the teacher and student(s) may collaboratively determine what strategy or set of strategies will be targeted for development, or the teacher may select a strategy for instruction. The teacher and students conference to discuss the significance and benefits of the strategy(s) to be mastered. The importance of student effort in strategy mastery is also established. This emphasis on metacognitive knowledge about the strategy and on student effort helps to set the stage for development of positive attitudes about writing. The goals of strategy instruction are discussed and determined. This stage enables students to make a commitment to strategy mastery and to participation as a partner/ collaborator, and helps to establish motivation.

If appropriate or desirable, the teacher may also examine current performance on the targeted composition skill with each individual student, perhaps looking through the student's writing portfolio or focusing on a couple of current compositions. Negative or ineffective self-statements (such as "I'm no good at this," or "I hate writing") and/or strategies the student has been using might also be discussed. If current performance is examined to help set the stage for strategy instruction, this should be done in a positive, collaborative manner. In addition, if current performance is discussed, the teacher and student may graph aspects of the compositions to be addressed in strategy instruction. For example, if a teacher and her students decide to use a prewriting, planning strategy based on story grammar, the number of story grammar elements evident in a few of each student's recent or selected compositions might be graphed. Graphing of current performance can help set the stage for both goal setting and self-monitoring.

Stage 3: Discussion of the Composition Strategy

During this stage, the teacher describes the composition strategy (such as recursive steps in prewriting or revision), explaining each step and any mnemonics involved in its use. Through discussion, the teacher helps the students to establish the advantages and benefits of the strategy. The teacher and students also discuss how and when to use the strategy. This discussion need not be limited to the writing task at hand; at this time students may begin to identify opportunities to use the stategy in new situations or for different tasks. However, the teacher should be sure that the proposed benefits of the strategy are expressed reasonably; they should not be exaggerated to avoid setting up unreasonable expectations. The important role of student effort in strategy mastery should also be communicated and understood by the student.

Stage 4: Modeling of the Composition Strategy and Self-Instructions

The teacher or a peer models the composition strategy and selected types of self-instructions (any or all of the types discussed in Chapter 4) while writing an actual composition during this stage. It is important that the modeling be natural and enthusiastic and that the self-statements have appropriate phrasing and inflection. The self-instructions modeled should be matched to the students' verbal style and language. If students will initially use prompts, such as charts listing the strategy steps or detailing a mnemonic, the model should use them also. After self-regulated use of the composition strategy has been modeled, the teacher and students should discuss the importance of the things people say to themselves while they work, and should identify together the types of self-instructions used by the model. Each student should then generate and record her or his own self-instructions, including each of the modeled types and any others he or she feels will be useful. These self-instructions will be used in later steps; modeling and re-explanation by the teacher can occur as needed. At this point, the teacher and students can also discuss the strategy steps and instructional components and collaboratively decide if any changes are needed to make the strategy more effective or efficient.

A detailed discussion of the development and use of self-instructions is presented in Chapter 4; the guidelines presented there should be used here. As noted in Chapter 4, alternatives to speaking out loud are possible for students who dislike overt verbalization. In addition, alternatives to live models are possible. We have success-fully used videotapes of peer models to introduce and model a target strategy. Teachers with whom we have worked have used other alternatives, as well. One teacher who was uncomfortable with modeling from memory or from notes on her lesson plan when she first began doing strategy instruction came up with an innovative approach that worked well for her and her students. She worked out a modeling script for a prewriting planning strategy, making sure that she had all of the components, steps, and types of self-instruc-tions she wished to model. She then put her self-talk on audio tape, reading from the script but talking naturally and appropriately. She played this tape with her writing group, using the overhead projector to complete the prewriting planning strategy as they went. When the modeling of the prewriting strategy was completed, she and her students collaboratively wrote the actual composition, using the pre-writing notes she had generated while modeling. Next they engaged in the type of discussion noted above. Finally, the students worked together to construct a bulletin board regarding the strategy, and made individual cue cards.

One of the aspects of modeling that makes it such a powerful procedure is the extent to which the model's performance can be individualized to meet the needs of a particular student or group of students. When teachers first begin cognitive modeling for their students, they often find it helpful to brainstorm together on the possible content of the model's performance. As teachers become more practiced and adept at modeling, they find the preparation for this stage much easier. The next section presents three different modeling scripts developed by three groups of teachers during a workshop we conducted. Each group first identified and discussed a particular student or group of students for whom the modeling would be intended, and identified particular needs or goals relevant to this individual or group. The same picture was used by each group as a story prompt, in order to facilitate comparing and contrasting the different scripts (pictures may or may not actually be used during instruction as story starters; we typically prefer that students have their own choice of topic). Each group then developed a script for modeling a prewriting, planning strategy involving the seven parts of a typical story (story grammar). As can be seen, the scripts differ in ways that make them responsive to the needs of the target students, yet each script is based on the same prewriting strategy.

Stage 5: Mastery of the Strategy

During this stage, students are required to memorize the steps in the composition strategy and the meaning of any mnemonics used either to represent the strategy steps or some part of the steps. Once the strategy is memorized, students can paraphrase as long as meaning remains intact. Students are also asked to memorize examples of each type of self-instruction from the personal lists they generated in Stage 4. Students can be prompted to use these statements in varying, appropriate contexts throughout the first five stages of strategy instruction; use of these self-statements will then come more easily in the next stage.

Stage 6: Collaborative Practice

At this point additional self-regulation procedures, such as goal setting, self-monitoring, or self-reinforcement, can be discussed, determined, and initiated (see Chapter 4). These components help to support motivation, maintenance and generalization, and cognitive and affective change. During this stage students employ the strategy, self-instructions, and any other self-regulation procedures as they actually compose. The teacher provides as much support and assistance as needed by individual students. Challenging, initial goals are determined cooperatively; criterion levels should be gradually increased until final goals are met. Prompts, interaction, and guidance are faded at a pace appropriate to individual students until strategy mastery is achieved. Throughout this stage the teacher and students plan for and initiate transfer and maintenance of the strategy. This stage may take more time than any of the others; students need to be given adequate time and support to master the strategy.

Stage 7: Independent Performance

If students have not already made the transition to use of covert self-instructions, this is encouraged at this stage as students now use the strategy independently. Self-regulation procedures are continued, but can be gradually faded as determined by the teacher and individual students. Plans for maintenance and generalization continue to be implemented, including booster sessions, and the teacher and students collaboratively evaluate strategy effectiveness and performance (as discussed further in Chapter 6).

Metascript

As we noted, the acquisition stages in our self-regulated strategy development model represent a "metascript," providing a general format and guidelines. We believe that it is important for teachers to personalize and individualize strategy instruction to meet both the needs of their students and their own preferences and needs. Various models for implementing strategy instruction have been developed, but there is little research supporting one method over another. There is also little research indicating which components are most critical, although initial research by ourselves and others indicates that a full-blown approach such as this is most effective with students who are experiencing problems in an academic area. In addition, a multicomponent approach such as this appears to facilitate longer-term maintenance and generalization. Enhancing maintenance and generalization is discussed further in Chapter 5.

There are many ways in which the acquisition and management stages we have presented can be reordered, combined, and recursive. For example, in some instances Stage I (Preskill Development) may not be needed at all. Or, Stage 5 (Mastery of the Strategy) might be combined with Stage 2 (Discussion of the Strategy); this may be particularly appropriate when students have had previous strategy instruction, the strategy is complicated, and the teacher wants to be sure of some degree of strategy mastery before modeling in order to enhance the effects of modeling. In some instances, teachers we have worked with have chosen to introduce self-instructions, or some subset of self- instructions, in Stage 3 (Discussion of the Strategy), rather than waiting until Stage 4 (Modeling). The additional self-regulation procedures introduced in Stage 6 could be introduced in earlier stages.

Recently, one of the teachers we worked with used an innovative approach: she combined Stages 4 (Modeling) and 6 (Collaborative Practice). Her middle school students had previously engaged in strategy instruction, and the strategy they were working on was a developmental extension of one the students had mastered (this strategy had been validated by a local group of teachers). She believed that combining these two stages would work and be more efficient. After discussion of the new strategy, she used it to plan and then create her own composition (a persuasive essay) while the students followed the same strategy steps to plan and write their own essays. If she had asked our opinion, we probably would have recommended against this combination of stages. Luckily, she did not ask our opinion, and our observations of her lesson and her students' essays indicated this process worked well. In fact, we were so intrigued by her approach we captured her next class session (continued Collaborative Practice combined with Modeling) on videotape.

Finally, we need to note that the stages we have presented do not necessarily correspond to individual lessons. In fact, as can be seen in Figure 1, in terms of lesson planning we typically combine the stages. Stages 1 and 2 are frequently combined into one lesson plan; Stages 3, 4, and 5 often constitute the second lesson plan; the third lesson plan typically covers Stages 4, 5, and 6 (modeling of the strategy is often done more than once, and mastery of the strategy may take some time); the fourth and fifth lesson plans focus on Stage 7 (independent performance is gradually developed and plans for maintenance and generalization are further implemented, as discussed previously). Further, teachers and students take as many class periods as necessary to complete any given lesson plan (lesson plan one may take only one class period, while lesson plans 2-5 may take several class periods to complete). Teachers are encouraged to combine, reorder, and plan in ways that work best for them.

Sample Teacher Modeling Scripts

The following three scripts were devised by three groups of teachers; each group identified students for whom the modeling was constructed.

Script 1: Developed for a small group of 4th grade students; of concern was that two students experienced a great deal of frustration with writing and often "gave up" writing before finishing their compositions.

What am I supposed to do? I am supposed to follow the five writing steps for a story.

1. I need to look at the picture first.

2. Next I need to brainstorm for ideas. I need for my mind to be free. I need to think of all the ideas I can. If I try, I can do this. This looks like... three people sitting around boxes, eating lo mein.

3. Next I need to write down the story reminder: W-W-W, What=2, How=2. I'm really having a good time. I like to use my imagination.

4. Step 4 is to fill in my reminder. The first W is who? Who is the main character? The kid. Who are the other characters? The mother and father. No. That's not exciting. I'm going to make it an aunt and uncle. Let's see. Now, the next W is when? Boy, this sure is taking a long time. But when I finish it, I'll be really proud. When does the story take place? The story takes place at night. It's dark. They're eating dinner.

    The next W is where does the story take place? Hmm. Is this their old house or new house? Are they going or coming? I think the aunt and uncle are moving into a new house right next door to the kid's house. Good, now this is getting easier.

    What=2. What does that mean? The first **what** is what does the main character want to do. The little boy is hoping his aunt and uncle let him stay the night to play in the boxes and sleep on the floor. The other **what** is what happens when he tries to do it. He finishes his dinner, doesn't spill anything, is polite. They say okay. The little boy is going to stay the night, plays in the wooden crates and gets stuck. Okay, I'm rolling now.

    The next step is How=2. The first **how** is how does the story end. The story ends when the aunt and uncle call the fire department. They come and cut the crate with an ax. I'm almost done now. I'm doing a good job. Last **H** is how does the main character feel. The little boy was really scared but now he is relieved and decides to go home for the night. Wow, that sure took me a long time, but I did it. I knew I could if I tried.

5. Now all I have to do is write the story.

The Story. My aunt and uncle are moving into the house next door to me. I'm having Chinese dinner with them. I hope they will let me stay for the night. I'll be real polite.

They are going to let me stay! I play in the empty wooden crates, but I get stuck. My aunt and uncle call the police who ax the crate open. I decide to go home to my house. My aunt's house is too exciting.

Let's see. Does my story have all the parts? Yes, it will have all the Ws and W=2 and H=2. Does my story make sense? Yes it does. It happened to my little brother so I know it makes sense. I did my best. I think I'll give a copy of this to my brother.

Script 2: Developed specifically for a 5th grade, male student with learning disabilities; this student has difficulty with reading and becomes anxious and frustrated with writing, but loves math, science, and to tell stories. To help with the student's level of anxiety, modeling was done slowly and calmly.

(Review the five writing steps on chart first, then model:) What is it I have to do? I have to write a story that will be fun for my friends to read. Relax, take my time.

What is my first step? I need to look at the picture and decide what is happening. The family in the picture is eating Chinese food in their house. It looks like they just moved. They must be hungry. Good. I think I know what I'll write. Now I must really concentrate. This is going to be the best story ever.

What are the story parts? (see chart) W-W-W; What=2; How=2. First, who are the main characters? I'll name them Mr. and Mrs. Wiz and their son Gerald, who's nickname is Gee. When is the story happening? It is a Saturday in September. Where does the story take place? They have just moved to Florida right next to Disney World. Mr. Wiz works for Disney and Gee loves Space Mountain. Mrs. Wiz is a semi-pro golfer (like my mom).

What is it that I have to do next? What=2. I don't need to rush or worry—stay calm and go slowly. What do they want to do? They want to eat, unpack, and get settled into their new house. What happens? They finish eating and go to unpack the china when a ghost jumps out of the box. Who's Gee Wiz gonna call? Ghostbusters? Wow, this is great! The Ghostbusters' line is busy, so the Wizzes jump on their three-seater 1972 Harley Low Rider. I can add more to this later.

What will the Wizzes do when they get to the Ghostbusters Office? First they ring the doorbell and this green slime runs over Mrs. Wiz's hand. She screams! Ooo, this is neat, but I've got to get back to the main idea. Egon, one of the ghostbusters, answers the door. "Hello. Ghostbusters. What can I do to help you?" Egon asks. Gee Wiz grabs Egon's leg and screams. "There's a ghost in our house." Mr. Wiz calmly says, "We need your help, now." Egon quickly sets off the Ghostbuster alarm and all the Ghostbusters get ready for the assignment. The Wizzes lead the way to their new house. OK, I have good notes for this part.

The next step is how does the story end? They get the ghost out of their new house? How will they do it?

The Ghostbusters chase the ghost in and out of every room. Egon whispers to the other Ghostbusters, "We've got to corner him in the basement; it's our only hope. We've got to make the ghost think he's chasing us." Everyone runs down the stairs to the basement, screaming and yelling as if they were afraid of the ghost. The ghost quickly glides after them, hooting and hollering. Just as the ghost is about to corner them, the Ghostbusters turn on their blasters, open the trap and zap the ghost into the trap. Everyone could hear the ghost screaming, "I'll get you yet!" "Yea!" shouted the Wizzes. "Thank you," replied the Ghostbusters, and off they drove, leaving the relieved and happy Wizzes at their new house.

How do the main characters feel? Gee Wiz is really disappointed because he could not have a pet ghost. Mr. and Mrs. Wiz, on the other hand, are pleased as punch that their house is ghost free. The Wizzes happily continue to unpack.

Let me check my steps. Did I complete each? Yes. My notes are good to start with. I could probably work on the ending a little more. Now I can start writing my story (write story with student's help).

Script 3: Developed for a small group of students experiencing severe problems with composition; none of these students has written a complete story.

What is it I have to do? - Write a story.

What is my first step? - Look at the picture and let my mind be free.

What do I see - I'll make a list.

1. I see — People: Mother, father, child.

2. What are they doing? — eating.

3. Where are they eating? — at home.

4. Home doesn't look right does it? No.

5. Maybe they just moved in — sounds good.

6. I don't see anything else right now. Let's see if I can write a story — OK?

Now I need my story part reminder. One step at a time.

W — who is the main character — the little boy (teacher makes notes) who else is in the story — mother, father

W — When does the story take place — Hmm, I think I'll look at the picture. I see a window. It's dark outside — must be at night.

W — Looking at the picture, it looks like they moved into a new house.

Now I need What=2. What does the main character want to do? Hmm, my main character is the little boy and he is trying to eat. What happens when he tries to do it? Hmmm, let's look at the picture. What do I see the boy doing? He is trying to get the food before his mother gives it to him. Mom doesn't look mad. Maybe they were both going for the last piece of food and the boy got it first. I like that. Let's look at the story part reminder.

Now I need, How=2—How does the story end? The boy says, "Boy that was a good dinner." I think that says it all. How does the main character feel? Hmmm. The boy feels full and sleepy.

Now I think I'm ready to write my story. First thing I'll do is look at the five writing steps.

1. Look at the picture — yes, I did. It is about a family eating dinner.

2. Let my mind be free — I did a lot of brainstorming.

3. Write down the story part reminder — I got it right here.

4. Write down story ideas for each part — Yes, I did it!

5. Now I'll write the story.

The Last Morsel

This story is about a boy and his mother and father. [That sounds good. Look at the story part reminder and see what the next part is.] It's dark outside and they just moved into a new house. [looks fine] [What happens?] He is trying to eat and he and his mother are both going for the last piece of food. [OK. I know now what to write.] The boy tells his mother, "Ha, I beat you." His mother starts to laugh. [I like that. Ok. Now I can finish this story.] The boy finishes his dinner and says, "That was good. Now I'm ready for bed." [Now I need a title. What's another word for food — morsel. Yes, I like that. How about this — The Last Morsel.]

Characteristics of Effective Strategy Instruction

As we have noted, effective strategy instruction typically has several components. Our work with teachers and students, however, has indicated to us that the *characteristics* of strategy instruction must also be carefully considered. Thus, we next discuss six major characteristics evident in our self-regulated strategy development model; we believe that these characteristics are critical to the success of this instructional approach.

Individualization. Cognitive strategy instruction can be done effectively either individually or in groups (including the whole class where appropriate). Whether instruction occurs individually or in groups, the preskills, skills, strategies, and self-regulation procedures to be developed should be responsive to the teacher's understanding of the learner and the task and tailored to students' capabilities (this is discussed further in Chapter 5). When the self-regulation and composition strategies to be learned are appropriate for a group of students, aspects of the instruction can be individualized. For example, it is important that students develop their own self-instructions in their own words, as discussed in Chapter 4. This can be done in a group situation by modeling and discussing types and purposes of self-instructions, and then having each student develop her or his own self-statements. Or, students might pair up or work as a group to help each other determine self-statements.

It is important that students progress through the stages of strategy acquisition at their own pace. Thus, at times the group may break down into smaller groups or the teacher may need to work individually with some students. Students who master the strategy more quickly than their peers may act as peer tutors or provide support and assistance to others. Finally, while a group of students may be working on mastering a particular set of composition and self-regulation strategies, goals can be individualized. Product and process composition goals might be determined individually, if appropriate (see Chapter 4). Cognitive and affective goals can also be tailored to individual student needs: one student may be using self-statements aimed at adopting a more reflexive style and coping with frustration, while another student's self-speech is focused on developing a more internal locus of control and a stronger sense of self-efficacy. The teacher can also provide individually tailored feedback and reinforcement to facilitate such goals, as well as to help students recognize improvements in performance and the usefulness of strategy instruction. Ongoing self-evaluation, using techniques such as self-monitoring or portfolio assessment, can also foster individualization.

Collaboration. Throughout this book we emphasize the importance of interactive instruction and the student's role as an active collaborator. While the teacher initially provides whatever degree of scaffolding or support needed, responsibility for recruiting, executing, monitoring, and modifying strategies is gradually transferred to the student. To facilitate this transfer, students can collaborate in such areas as the selection and determination of goals, the implementation, evaluation, and modification of the strategies and strategy acquisition procedures, and planning for maintenance and generalization. Collaboration in areas such as these facilitates autonomous, reflective, strategic performance. The areas and ways in which students can collaborate are limited only by the imaginations and willingness of teachers and students.

Mastery-based instruction. Strategy instruction focuses on targeted affective, cognitive, and composition goals rather than on abstract dimensions or presumed underlying deficits. Instruction to meet these goals should be mastery-based: students should proceed through the stages of instruction at their own pace and should not proceed from one stage to the next until they have met reasonable criteria for doing so. This need not imply 100% mastery at each stage of strategy instruction. Rather, the stages are frequently recursive — teachers may return to any stage at any time, with criteria for progression becoming higher as the student recycles through the stages. For example, preskill development is an early stage in our instructional model. However, students need not fully master preskills before going on to the next stages; preskill development can continue throughout the first four or five stages until mastery is reached. However, students should achieve a high level of preskill mastery before the later stages of strategy instruction, such as mastering strategy steps and engaging in collaborative practice. If mastery of a particular stage or skill is taking an inordinate amount of time, then the teacher should reconsider what is being taught and how it is being taught.

Anticipatory instruction. Basically what we mean here is that multiple aspects of strategy instruction are well thought out and planned for in advance. We have already noted that generalization and maintenance should be planned for and initiated from the very beginning of instruction (this is discussed further in Chapter 5). In addition, we attempt to do what we refer to as "anticipating glitches." As we and the teachers with whom we work plan to implement strategy instruction for the first time or in a new area, we brainstorm things that could go wrong or prove difficult, particularly in light of our understanding of the learner and the composition task. This sort of thinking ahead helps us to avoid or be ready for difficulties as they arise, even if they are not the difficulties we anticipated. Once students become involved in the planning and implementation of strategy instruction, we also involve them in anticipating glitches. Thus, difficulties and failures are anticipated and subsumed into the instructional program. We find that routine review of earlier stages of instruction, as well as booster sessions once formal strategy instruction is completed, are also helpful here.

Booster sessions are particularly important as a form of "relapse prevention." Booster sessions should be collaboratively planned for in advance; at the end of formal strategy mastery, the teacher and students should discuss a plan for keeping the strategy alive. As part of this plan, booster sessions can be anticipated or even scheduled. A booster session can consist of elements such as the following:

1. reviewing or renewing self-regulation procedures such as goal setting or self-monitoring;

2. reviewing the strategies mastered;

3. collaborative practicing of the mastered strategies;

4. discussing any changes in a strategy or use of a strategy on the students' part (the teacher should be alert to changes that subvert or weaken the strategy, as well as improvements);

5. collaborative problem solving regarding any problems the students have experienced with a strategy or adaptations of a strategy across the curriculum;

6. discussing of successful experiences with strategy use or generalization;

7. continued planning for anticipated glitches; and any other appropriate activities determined by teachers and students.

Enthusiastic teachers working within a support network. Enthusiastic, responsive teaching is an integral part of strategy instruction. As we have stressed earlier in this chapter, the teacher plays an important role in helping students understand the meaning and efficacy of strategies as well as their own efforts. In addition to establishing the credibility of strategies, teachers also need to serve as models of self-regulated, strategic performance, and establish a collaborative, supportive environment for strategy mastery and autonomous, reflective learning.

Given the complexity of strategy instruction, however, individual, enthusiastic teachers operating alone will face greater difficulty with successful implementation than will those operating from a sound support base. We have found that understanding and implementing strategy instruction is much easier for teachers when they work together with other teachers to learn the processes involved and have opportunities to share both successes and failures. Further, the impact of instruction on students will be much greater when there is a critical mass of teachers implementing strategy instruction within the same school or district. Such a group of teachers can work to maintain and generalize strategic performance across the curriculum and grades. Finally, principals, learning specialists, and other school administrators play a critical role in providing leadership and support for the nurturing of an instructional environment geared toward self-directed learning. Organizational support is an important factor in successful strategy instruction.

Developmental enhancement. To teach a strategy well, teachers need to understand and help students come to see the meaning and the significance of the strategy, as well as its strengths and weaknesses (in other words, to develop metastrategy knowledge). This requires an understanding of where the strategy(s) to be taught fits in the larger scheme of things in terms of the student's development both as a writer and as a self-directed learner. The teacher needs to understand the many ways in which the strategy can empower the writer, in order to help students take full advantage of the tool they are mastering.

A skillful, effective writer employs strategies and conventions of the craft the way a jazz musician uses a melody. The mature writer is able to profit from the variations, the riffs, the twists, and ultimately the meaning of the strategies and conventions of writing. Thus, as writers mature, they continually refine, combine, and enhance the strategies they have mastered or created, using them in more sophisticated ways. Teachers can facilitate this process by collaboratively planning for and supporting among their students the developmental enhancement of strategies and strategic performance.

To illustrate, suppose that a teacher is preparing to begin strategy instruction in story writing. She and her students collaboratively determine that a prewriting planning strategy based on story grammar would be desirable; that is, a strategy that would help students to craft the basic components of a story (characters, locale, time, starter event, goal, action, ending, and reaction) before they begin writing. These parts can then be elaborated upon or revised during writing. Among the strengths of this strategy are increased prewriting planning and problem solving, more complete and detailed stories, and an enhanced understanding of the nature of a typical story. The teacher knows, however, that the strategy to be taught has its limitations. While this seven-part story grammar is common in Western culture, other story grammars exist in both Western and other cultures. Thus, once students have mastered this strategy, she plans to introduce them to other story telling structures, such as those used by African tribal storytellers, or stories that focus in-depth on one or two characters rather than on actions and reactions. She will then engage her students' cooperation in determining further story grammars they would like to experience as writers, and in developing strategies for these story grammars as necessary and appropriate.

Further, suppose that this teacher has engaged in cooperative curriculum and strategy instruction planning with the teachers who will work with these students in the coming years. She knows, therefore, that not only will further developmental enhancement of this initial strategy occur over time, but that additional writing strategies, such as brainstorming strategies, creative writing strategies, and yet other story grammar strategies, will be created, developed, and mastered by these students and their teachers (including herself) as the students mature. This knowledge allows her to create powerful linkages between and among the strategies her students master, not only in writing but across the curriculum. Strategy determination should be embedded within this sort of vision, and it is toward this vision that we are working.

THE STORY GRAMMAR STRATEGY: AN ILLUSTRATION

Here we provide an illustration of how one teacher used these strategy acquisition and management procedures to help her students master the story grammar strategy.[1] This teacher, Barbara Danoff, was working with a group of fifth grade students (including both normally achieving students and several students with learning disabilities) during Writers' Workshop. Writers' Workshop is a process approach to writing instruction; students had one class period a day devoted to this. Most of the students Barbara was working with had been in Writers' Workshop for the past three years. Thus, these students were used to choosing their own topics and genre, determining the content and purpose of their writing, selecting pieces for completion and publication, using peers and teacher as a resource, and peer editing.

Barbara carefully considered both the learners in this group and story writing as a composition task. Barbara's reading of the stories that the students had written indicated to her that some of the students used all seven common story parts, but that most of the students commonly neglected two or more story parts. Further, all of the students, including those who used all of the parts, could improve their story writing by including greater detail and elaboration, as well as more goals and actions. Barbara also considered the affective and cognitive characteristics of the individual students in this group; she had been working with these students for the past two years and thus had the advantage of knowing them well. Most of the students enjoyed writing and were comfortable with it; a few of the students (including a couple of students who were identified as learning disabled and a couple who were not), however, still evidenced anxiety about composing as well as writing difficulties. These students needed a stronger sense of motivation, enhanced self-efficacy, and more internal attributions (what Barbara termed overall an "I can do this if I try" attitude). Finally, Barbara knew that these students would be going to middle school the following year, where they would face increased demands for writing products, such as book reports and biographies, that could be informed by knowledge and use of story grammar. She also felt that such knowledge could benefit many of the students in terms of reading comprehension.

Thus, Barbara decided to offer these students instruction on the story grammar strategy within the process approach used in Writers' Workshop. She wanted to make it possible for her students to master the story grammar strategy and thus grow as writers, yet continue to maintain control over the content and purpose of their stories and to use the strategy within the writers' community already established (using peers as a resource, peer editing, publication, and so on). The story grammar strategy and the story grammar mnemonic are presented in Table 2-2. This strategy is designed to enhance advanced planning and content generation. This strategy, however, is not meant to be used as a formula for story content. Where, when, and how the story parts are introduced, used, and developed is up to the individual student; sophistication in terms of these aspects of the parts develops as writers mature.

Barbara decided to follow the seven stages typically used in self-instructional strategy development, with a few modifications. For example, she reversed the order of Stages 1 and 2. She also decided to incorporate goal setting (on an individual basis), self-monitoring (including self-assessment and self-recording), and self-reinforcement as part of the strategy acquisition and management procedures. Barbara planned and conducted her instruction as follows:

Table 2-2. The Story Grammar Strategy Steps

1. Think of a story that you would like to share with others.
2. Let your mind be free.
3. Write down the story part reminder:

    W-W-W

    What = 2

    How = 2

4. Make notes of your ideas for each part.
5. Write your story— use good parts, add, elaborate, or revise as you write or afterwards, and make sense.

The Story Grammar Mnemonic

Who is the main character; who else is in the story?

When does the story take place?

Where does the story take place?

What does the main character do or want to do; what do other characters do?

What happens when the main character does or tries to do it?

 What happens with other characters?

How does the story end?

How does the main character feel; how do other characters feel?

Stage 1: Initial Conference—Instructional Goals and Significance. Barbara decided to begin with a conference in order to offer the strategy instruction to her students and then work with those who chose to learn the story grammar strategy at this time. During this conference, she and the students discussed the common parts of a story, the goal of story grammar strategy instruction (to write better stories—ones that are more fun for you to write and more fun for others to read), and how inclusion and expansion of the story grammar elements can improve a story. Barbara also briefly outlined the instructional procedures that would be followed to help the students master the strategy, and stressed the students' roles as collaborators during strategy mastery, implementation, and evaluation (including the possibility of acting as a peer tutor for other students who wished to learn this strategy in the future). The importance of student effort in strategy mastery was stressed. Perhaps because of her enthusiasm or the way she explained the strategy instruction, all of the students opted to participate in the strategy instruction.

Stage 2: Preskill development. Barbara knew that her students were comfortable with the vocabulary involved in the story grammar strategy and mnemonic. Thus, she decided to focus on the story grammar mnemonic itself during preskill development. She did this in several ways (each student was given a small chart that provided the story grammar mnemonic, as seen in Table 2). First, after discussing the meaning of each element, students identified story grammar elements in literature they were currently reading for fun or in other classes. Because Barbara wanted students to generalize their understanding of story grammar to reading comprehension, she spent some time discussing how, when we read the writing of others, we can use story grammar to help us get their meaning. In addition, the different ways in which different authors developed or used story parts were highlighted. Next, the students generated ideas for story parts as a group, using a story idea offered by a student, a picture, or other story origins. Barbara explained to the students that they needed to memorize the mnemonic, and provided practice in several ways (chart present and absent, rehearsal, partner testing, etc.). Finally, Barbara had each student select two or three of their stories that had been written previously, and determine which of the story grammar elements were present in each story. She met individually with each student to explain and demonstrate graphing of the number of story grammar elements in each story, and to discuss how they would continue to use the graph for self-recording throughout instruction. With those students whose graphs indicated that they typically used all or nearly all of the story parts, Barbara discussed with them how they could improve their parts with detail, elaboration, and more action.

Stage 3: Discussion of the composition strategy. Barbara introduced the five-step story grammar strategy to her group of students using the overhead projector; each student was given a small chart with the five steps on it as well. Barbara and her students discussed the five steps; she asked her students to tell her what they thought the reason was for each step. Next the group discussed how and when to use the strategy. While the discussion began with story writing, Barbara also asked them to consider other times they might use it. Linkages to writing book reports, biographies, and to reading were discussed. Barbara further established the point that strategies cannot work without having been mastered and emphasized the role of student effort in strategy mastery and management. Finally, Barbara decided to introduce one form of self-instruction at this point: creativity self-statements. She modeled for the students how she often used statements to herself to free up her mind and think of good story ideas and parts. The self-statements she modeled included: "Let my mind be free," "Think of fun ideas," "Think of something no one else might think of," and "Take my time, good ideas will come to me." Some of the students offered examples of their own self-statements. After discussing how these self-statements were helpful, the students generated their own preferred creativity self-statements, recorded them on paper, and practiced using these self-statements to generate story parts.

Stage 4: Modeling the composition strategy and self-instructions. Barbara asked her students to get out their strategy mnemonic and strategy steps charts and their lists of self-statements. She then shared a story idea with them that she had been thinking about using, and began modeling use of the story grammar strategy by planning and writing a story while "thinking out loud." She encouraged the students to help her as she planned and made notes for each story part, and as she wrote a first draft of her story (changes or additions to her plans were made as she wrote). She modeled five additional types of self-instructions while composing: problem definition (What is it I have to do? I need to...), planning (including use of each of the five strategy steps), self-evaluation (How am I doing, am I using each step, can I think of more details?), self-reinforcement (I really like this idea.), and coping (I can do this if I try; Don't worry, worry doesn't help; Take my time.) After completing the story, the group again discussed the importance of what we say to ourselves while we work and identified the types of self-statements the teacher had used. The students provided examples of personal positive (and negative, if volunteered) self-statements and then generated and recorded their own examples of the types of self-instructions. Finally, Barbara asked the students to consider the strategy steps and mnemonic and to suggest any changes they thought were needed to make the strategy more effective or efficient. The students did not suggest any changes; Barbara asked them to continue considering this as they worked with the strategy.

Stage 5: Mastery of the strategy. Barbara asked her students to practice the five-step strategy alone or with a partner in any way they liked, and noted the importance of memorizing the strategy (paraphrasing was allowed as long as meaning remained intact). She also asked the students to memorize examples of each type of self-instruction from their personal lists. Some of the students memorized the steps, mnemonic, and self-statements easily, while others had more difficulty. At this point, instruction continued on an individual basis. Barbara moved into collaborative practice with each student when she and the student determined that they were ready to do so. Perfect recall of the strategy steps, mnemonic, and self-statements was not always necessary for beginning collaborative practice, as Barbara explained that memorization of these things could continue as collaborative practice progressed. Barbara prompted individual students to use their self-statements both during writing time and at other appropriate times; this continued throughout instruction and afterwards as well.

Stage 6: Collaborative practice. Barbara initiated goal setting, self-monitoring (continuing the graphs they had started in Stage 2), and self-reinforcement with each individual student as he or she began collaborative practice. (In some instances, two or more students were ready to begin at the same time and she was able to introduce these self-regulation procedures to them as a small group.) The goal for each student was to include all seven story parts. Barbara believed this to be a proximal goal (initial but challenging, see Chapter 4) for all of the students; all of the students were able to meet this goal once they had mastered the strategy. Each time a student completed a story, Barbara and the student independently counted the number of story parts included, compared counts, graphed the number on the student's graph, and compared this number to the goal set previously. Self-reinforcement was encouraged when students met or came close to their goals. Barbara also provided social reinforcement; concrete, external reinforcement was not used at all.

Story writing during this stage began with Barbara collaboratively planning a story with each student; each student then wrote her or his story independently. Barbara made sure each student was using the strategy steps and mnemonic. She modified her input and support to meet the individual needs of each student; with some students she provided a great deal of prompting, guidance, and support, while others needed very little. Prompts (the charts and self-statement lists), guidance, and support were faded at a pace appropriate to individual students, and Barbara began encouraging students to use covert self-speech. Barbara found that this took less time than she had anticipated, however, and most students were ready for independent performance after two or three collaborative experiences.

Also during this stage, Barbara had a conference with all of the students together to discuss and plan for strategy maintenance and generalization. The students decided upon review and booster sessions as necessary to help them maintain strategic performance, and discussed opportunities they might have for generalization (one student reported using the strategy in English class when reading stories, while another reported using the strategy to help write outlines; several students mentioned writing stories at home). Finally, throughout this stage the students were available to each other as a resource or for peer editing, as they had typically done during Writers' Workshop.

Stage 7: Independent performance. Students now independently planned and composed stories using the five-step strategy and self-instructional statements (at this point, students typically used fewer self-instructions than they had in earlier stages; this was appropriate as strategy use was beginning to become automatic). Barbara provided positive and constructive feedback as appropriate to each individual student and continued to encourage the use of covert self-instructions. Students were asked to use the charts only if necessary and to try to write without them; continued use of planning on paper was encouraged. Most of the students did not use the charts at all, but rather simply used sheets of paper to record the story grammar mnemonic and their initial ideas. Some students, however, no longer wrote out ideas for all of the story parts. These students told Barbara that they didn't need to because they had the parts in their heads and were ready to write. She told them this was fine, but to remember to check their drafts to be sure they had included all of the parts, as well as detail and elaboration.

Students continued the goal setting and self-monitoring procedures independently for two more stories, and then were told that use of these procedures for future stories was up to them. As students reached independent performance, they became available to help with collaborative practice with other students. Selection of writing genre during Writers' Workshop was now left up to the students; individuals engaged in story writing as well as other writing activities.

Once again, a group conference was held to evaluate the story grammar strategy and instruction. The students were pleased with the strategy and their use of it. Barbara initiated a discussion of the strategy's weaknesses at this point and explained to the students that other story structures did exist, such as that used by African tribal storytellers, and that the students might want to compare and contrast these story grammars or learn new story strategies in the future. The students indicated an interest in doing so. The importance of student control of the strategy, and creative use of the story parts in terms of when, where, and how they were used was stressed. The plans for maintenance were reviewed and Barbara indicated that she would periodically check with each student to see if they remembered the strategy and how they were using it; booster sessions would be scheduled if needed.

Generalization of the strategy and the self-instructions was also discussed again. Several students mentioned using the mnemonic in reading or for other writing assignments. One student reported using the mnemonic to write a "tall tale" in another teacher's class, while other students mentioned using it for journal writing and for writing for the school newspaper. These reports were confirmed by other teachers who reported to Barbara that some students were using both the mnemonic and some of their self-statements in their classes. One teacher noted that several students were using the mnemonic for both writing and revising. Barbara planned to continue to prompt generalization in writing as well as other areas of the curriculum.

IMPLEMENTATION AND EVALUATION

Implementation and evaluation of the strategy acquisition and management stages occur concurrently and reciprocally. Evaluation focuses not only on composition skills and processes, but also on cognitive and affective changes and development. Both formal and informal methods of evaluation in these areas are discussed in Chapter 6. Because evaluation is ongoing and formative as well as summative, changes can be made in the strategy or the instructional procedures as needed throughout instruction.

In the illustration involving Barbara's class, evaluation occurred throughout instruction and at the end. Students were involved in evaluation through the use of their graphs and in discussions about the strategy and instructional procedures. Barbara had taught this strategy previously and several changes had been made in the strategy and procedures in earlier years; no new changes were made by this group. Barbara also engaged in a form of portfolio assessment, looking through the students' earlier writings and comparing these with stories written during and after strategy instruction. Both she and her students found that strategy use meaningfully improved story writing. Barbara informally assessed students' attributions, attitudes toward writing and the use of strategies, and their views of themselves as writers through individual and group discussions. She felt that positive changes were occurring in these areas for nearly all of the students, particularly those who had been anxious about writing or critical of their abilities. Sample stories from Barbara's class follow.

Stories from Barbara's Class[1]

These two stories were written by Jill, a normally achieving student in Barbara's class, the first before and the second after strategy instruction[a]:

One day a boy went to a pond near his house. When he got to the pond he watched a frog jump around. Then the frog jumped over to the boy, they stared at each other. Suddenly the frog jumped away and the boy never saw him again.

Dreams! Dreams! Dreams!

Once there was a penguin named Rubin. There was nothing special about Rubin. He was just a black and white penguin. Rubin lived in the San Diego Zoo. He loved the zoo. Then one day he saw a boy that came to visit the zoo wearing shorts with sailboats on them. Rubin loved the shorts. Rubin also wanted them. That night Rubin had a dream. It was about Rubin getting the shorts. Once he got the shorts he had gotten a Walkman. Rubin dreamed that after he got the Walkman he turned it on and started to dance. Rubin danced all night in his dream. When Rubin got up he was sad because he had only dreamed it.

The End

These two stories were written by Christie, a student with learning disabilities in Barbara's class, the first before and the second after strategy instruction[b]:

A monkey named Joe was bored when he got up from his nap. His friend Fred was on the telephone with his boss. He was moping around the house for a half hour. Then he got hungry so he went in the kitchen to get something to eat. He saw Fred's wallet on the table. He picked it up and looked inside and saw money. He saw credit cards and lots of money. First he picked up the 100 dollar bill but it was old and written on the right so he put it down. Then he picked up a one dollar bill and it was brand new. Then his friend got off of the telephone and saw Joe with his dollar and said what are you doing? Joe just made a face.

Baseball and Tommy

One hot, humid day in April (April 22, 1990) there was Tommy, who lived in Maryland-Virginia. Tommy is a short boy, he is 9 years old with brown hair. And he loved to wear his red hat, blue jeans, and his gray sweatshirt. One afternoon Tommy saw his friends (Jim, Fred, Scott, Tod) were playing ball. But when he went home he tried to play but he was not good. He practiced and practiced, finally he was getting good. So when he told his friends they said, "Lets see how good you are." So they went to Tod's house and played in his backyard. It was a hot, humid day so they had to stop. They went in and got drinks. Then Scott said, "Hey, you're pretty good." "Thank you," Tommy said. When Tommy tried out for the team (neighborhood) he made it. When he got home he was so proud of himself. He told his father and his father said if you're so good then try out for the school team. The next day he watched the team and tried to learn the plays. When he went home he played with his friends, like the team. The next day he went in to talk with the coach and ask if he could try out. The coach said sure, we're looking for another player. So Tommy went for it and made the team. When he got home he told his father. His father was so proud he took him out for ice cream. Tommy's father said, "I am sorry for acting so rude before and being so forceful." Tommy said, "It's ok."

The End

The following story was written after strategy instruction by Vanessa who, although one of the more developed writers in the class, typically did not use all of the story parts in her pre-strategy instruction compositions; her goals during instruction also included using more elaboration, detail, and actions in her stories:

The St. Patrick's Day Leprechaun

One day in Doggy Land, Valerie (a poodle) was walking through the forest. It was March 31, 1990. Valerie was a white poodle with a green bow in her hair. Since it was St. Patrick's Day, Valerie was going to find a leprechaun.

She was skipping along when all of a sudden she heard a moan. Then she heard a whimper. Now, Valerie was a very curious dog. She started to walk east. That was where the sound was coming from. In surprise she found out that it was a dog too. He was tan and white with big, brown, sad eyes. He also had on a green top hat and a bow-tie with clovers on it. It was a leprechaun! Valerie said, "Why are you crying Mr. Leprechaun?"

"Because I have scratched my paw on a thorn bush! Could you please help me!" begged the leprechaun. Well, Valerie wanted a little something out of this too. So she said, "Only if you give me three wishes!"

"Oh, all right!" said Mr. Leprechaun. Valerie got a band-aid out of her purse and put it on the leprechaun. He felt much better. "Now what do you wish for?"

"I want a bike, a new dress, and a pot of gold!" said Valerie. Out of mid-air came a bike, and a new dress. "But where's my pot of gold?" asked Valerie.

"Well for that we'll have to go over the rainbow. Hop on!" shouted Mr. Leprechaun. Together they rode up onto the rainbow on the magic carpet. When they got on top they slid down. They landed on a cloud. Under a rock was the pot of gold.

After that Valerie went home. She laid her things down on the table. She was thirsty from the long ride. She went into the kitchen. When she came back her bike, dress, and pot of gold were gone. "Oh no!" thought Valerie. She ran back to the woods. But he wasn't there. She looked up at the sky. The rainbow was gone! For it was only her imagination.

The End

Barbara has also participated in research studies on the story grammar strategy with us, and we have collected both formal and informal assessments. Analyses of pre- and post-story grammar strategy instruction stories in her classroom one year indicated that students had shown improvement in the number of story parts included in their stories, (except for those few who were already using all of the parts, these students showed improvement in detail and action in their stories), as well as improvement in the quality of their writing. Quality ratings were obtained by having teachers blind to the conditions and nature of instruction provide holistic ratings for each story.

In addition to these formal measures, an interview was held with each student and with another teacher who was working with Barbara at the time. All of the students indicated that they believed the story grammar strategy had improved their writing. Those students who had already been using all of the parts noted that they now used greater detail and more action. The mnemonic was the aspect of instruction most frequently nominated as most enjoyable. One student commented, "The W-W-W, What=2, How=2 builds up your resources." None of the students indicated any problems in incorporating strategy instruction into the process approach (Writers' Workshop) being used in their school. The other teacher who was working with Barbara during Writers' Workshop that year said that as she worked with the students she could see "light bulbs going off." She mentioned that one student had commented to her, "Now this story writing makes sense." In short, although most of the students were already familiar with the parts of a story, mastery of the strategy helped them to understand what it was they knew.

In addition to this study of the complete group, we also selected six students whom we followed closely throughout instruction. Three of these students were learning disabled; the other three were normally achieving students. In addition to the findings above, the data collected indicated that the normally achieving and learning-disabled students all improved in terms of story parts and quality. Maintenance checks two and four weeks after instruction indicated that improvements were maintained. Generalization across teachers was obtained for four of the six students (one learning-disabled student and one normally achieving student needed further assistance to achieve this generalization). Perhaps most intriguing to us was the finding that Stages 1 through 5 alone resulted in some improvement in students' writing, but Stages 6 and 7 (Collaborative and Independent Practice) resulted in greater improvements. Barbara indicated that she felt Collaborative Practice was an important key in strategy mastery.

It is interesting to mention here how another teacher we have worked with, Richard Gorski, adapted the story grammar concept for use with his first-graders with severe reading problems. He modified the strategy and the instruction to fit with the story-retelling activities he was doing with his class. Richard and his students began with *The Three Billy Goats Gruff*, initially identifying the story parts who, when, and where. Other story parts were added later. The students made dioramas and did other art projects related to the retelling and the story components. Once the students were able to retell the story, using all of the components, they wrote and produced a play. It is our hope that the framework provided here will help teachers to develop their own personalized, individualized approach to strategy instruction.

In the next chapter we present a family of composition strategies which we have validated in classrooms like Barbara's. These strategies can be mastered using the acquisition and management stages we have discussed here, or through modifications appropriate to teachers' and students' needs. For some students, the strategies might be effectively and efficiently mastered with direct explanation of the strategy and how to use it. Other students may be able to master the strategy through the use of one or more of the self-regulation procedures presented in Chapter 4. Some students may develop effective strategies on their own, and will not need strategy instruction. As students' writing problems become more severe, however, the more explicit and multicomponent strategy instruction needs to be. These students will need greater support, such as that found in the strategy acquisition and management stages presented in this chapter, in order to integrate writing strategies, self-regulation strategies, and metastrategy knowledge. Planning for successful, multicomponent strategy instruction is discussed further in Chapter 5.

END NOTES

1.   We express our appreciation to Barbara Danoff, a special education teacher who works collaboratively with regular education teachers at Georgian Forest Elementary School, Maryland, for this illustration and for her work with us over the past few years in the development and refinement of the story grammar strategy.

a.   Stories have been corrected for spelling and punctuation.

b.   Christie was the student who reported using the story grammar strategy to help her write a "tall tale" in her literature class.

CHAPTER THREE

A Family of Writing Strategies

A family of writing strategies that we and our colleagues at the University of Maryland have developed are presented in this chapter, including strategies for planning the initial draft of a text as well as revising strategies. The "story grammar" strategy is not reexamined here, as it was covered in depth in the previous chapter.

A common format is used to examine each of the strategies. The rationale underlying the construction of the strategy is considered first. Instructional procedures relevant to teaching the strategy are then examined. Because the procedures for teaching writing strategies were illustrated in the preceding chapter, the comments in this section are specific to the strategy under consideration. Next, the power of the strategy is appraised by exploring how students and their writing changed following instruction. Finally, suggestions for how to modify or extend the strategy are presented.

We also consider how these strategies can be used in tandem and provide specific suggestions for teachers interested in developing their own writing strategies.

THE BRAINSTORMING STRATEGY: A PLANNING STRATEGY FOR GENERATING WRITING MATERIAL

The Brainstorming strategy was primarily designed to help children generate ideas and content to write about. One of the most persistent problems for young writers is finding enough to say. Even when writing about personal experiences, they often omit important events or run out of content. A few well-directed questions, however, often reveal that there was much more they could have said.

How can teachers help students gain access to the knowledge they have? One promising means is to have them "brainstorm" ideas in advance of writing. Listing possible words or ideas to use in a paper provides students with a means for carrying out a self-directed memory search. It helps them complete a survey of what they know, and thinking about one idea often stimulates the generation of other ideas.

Two types of content that students can generate in advance of writing include topical ideas ("say how I felt, tell what I did,...") or single words. For this strategy, we concentrated our efforts on helping students generate single words. When producing topical ideas there is a greater tendency for students to become bogged down in considering how each idea will be connected. The process of generating possible "things to say" then becomes short-circuited, because the student becomes involved with other demands.

Furthermore, we wanted students to "brainstorm" words that would have a strong chance of improving the quality of what they wrote. In reading children's stories, it struck us that their writing often lacked color because they failed to use words that were active and descriptive. It has also been well documented that the type and variety of vocabulary that students use in their writing is a powerful indicator of teachers' evaluations of writing quality. Thus, the strategy we designed helped students "brainstorm" action verbs, adjectives, and adverbs in advance of writing.

The Strategy

The strategy consisted of the following five steps:

- LOOK AT THE PICTURE AND WRITE DOWN GOOD WORDS FOR MY STORY.

- THINK OF A GOOD STORY IDEA TO USE MY WORDS IN.

- WRITE MY STORY — USE GOOD WORDS AND MAKE SURE MY STORY MAKES SENSE.

- READ BACK OVER MY STORY AND ASK MYSELF — DID I WRITE A GOOD STORY?

- FIX MY STORY — CAN I USE MORE GOOD WORDS?

While the strategy focuses on "brainstorming" good words (action verbs, adjectives, and adverbs) to use in the story, making sense and developing a good story line is emphasized throughout. Without this emphasis some children would undoubtedly decide that their goal in writing a story is to get as many of these words in as possible, forgetting that the primary goal in story writing is to communicate, inform, or entertain the audience.

It is also important to note that the first two steps in the strategy are not sequential. Rather, they should be applied recursively; writers may return to any stage at any time. The selection of a story line will influence the words selected, and the words selected can give the writer ideas for developing the story line. In addition, we used pictures (as reflected in the first step) to help students get started; other story starters, such as an opening sentence or the final sentence to a story, could be used as well, or students could select their own topic. Finally, the steps presented above represent the bare-bone prompts that students use to remind themselves to carry out activities. In the fourth step, for example, the writer reads the story to see if it makes sense. The writer does more than evaluate, however. If something doesn't make sense, it is revised.

Teaching The Strategy

In teaching the strategy, we typically start by having students first learn to use it when "brainstorming" action verbs to use in their story. After they can do this successfully, they practice using the strategy to generate adverbs; adjectives are added last.

During PRESKILL DEVELOPMENT, charts that provide a definition and examples can be used to introduce students to the types of words they will "brainstorm" (see Table 1). Instead of using grammatical terms, we used simpler and more descriptive words such as "describing words" (adjectives), "action words" (action verbs) and "action helpers" (adverbs).

We found this modest change to be helpful for students who are not especially adept with formal grammatical nomenclature. In fact, before we made this change, one young student informed us he could not do the strategy because he had "failed adjectives and adverbs" in his other class. When the strategy was reintroduced with an indication that brainstorming would involve describing and action words, he was confident that he could learn to use the strategy. Once students can independently generate at least three examples of each of the target words in response to a picture stimulus, the next step in instruction is initiated.

During the second stage, the INITIAL CONFERENCE, each student's performance on previous stories is examined and depicted on a graph the student keeps in a writing folder. The student and teacher separately count the number of action words included in three of the student's previous stories, compare counts, and resolve any differences.

At this point, students are asked to agree to work collaboratively with the teacher to learn the strategy. They also discuss that their goal is to write better stories, why this is important, and how incorporat-

Table 3-1. Charts for Action Words, Action Helpers, and Describing Words.

USE ACTION WORDS
ACTION WORDS TELL WHAT PEOPLE, THINGS, OR ANIMALS DO. THEY ARE *DOING* WORDS.

- HE *JUMPED* AND *SHOUTED* AT THE GAME.
- THE MAN *WORRIED* AND *THOUGHT* ABOUT HER.
- THE BOOK *FELL* ON THE FLOOR.
- THE HORSE *GALLOPED* DOWN THE ROAD.

USE ACTION HELPERS
ACTION HELPERS ARE WORDS THAT GO ALONG WITH ACTION WORDS. THEY HELP TELL MORE ABOUT THE ACTION. THEY TELL *HOW* THE ACTION IS DONE.

- THE DOG RAN *QUICKLY*.
- THE BOOK FELL *QUIETLY*.
- THE BOY RAN *FAST*.
- THE TAXI DROVE *SLOWLY*.
- THE MAN LAUGHED *LOUDLY*.
- SHE SMILED *HAPPILY*.
- THE SQUIRREL LOOKED *CAREFULLY*.
- HE POUNDED THE NAIL *HARD*.

*MANY ACTION HELPERS END IN *LY*, BUT NOT ALL DO.

USE DESCRIBING WORDS
DESCRIBING WORDS TELL MORE ABOUT PEOPLE, ANIMALS, PLACES, OR THINGS. THEY HELP TO PAINT A PICTURE. DESCRIBING WORDS MAY TELL ABOUT: COLOR, SHAPE, HOW MANY, SIZE, FEELINGS, SMELLS, SOUNDS, TASTE, ETC.

- THE *SICK* GIRL WENT HOME.
- THERE WERE *FIVE* BOXES.
- THE *PRETTY* LEAF WAS *RED*.
- THE *ROUGH* WOOD HURT HER *SORE* FEET.
- THE CITY WAS *DIRTY*.
- THE *BIG*, ROUND BOX IS MINE.
- THE BOY WAS *BRAVE*.
- I LIKE *SALTY* POPCORN.

ing action words, action helpers, and describing words improves a story. The instructor and students next discuss how to graph performance and why this self-monitoring procedure should be used with subsequent stories.

The teacher and students DISCUSS THE EXECUTIVE STRATEGY using a small chart, emphasizing the recursive nature of the various steps. The advantages of using the strategy, as well as how and when to use it, are discussed further. The teacher shares how he or she brainstorms using self-verbalizations such as: "take my time"; "good words will come to me"; and "let my mind be free." Students are asked to share verbalizations they would like to use. Discussion then focuses on why the things we say to ourselves are important. Students then generate their own statements which they record on paper and are asked to practice using them during writing as well as at any other times they are helpful.

As the teacher MODELS THE STRATEGY AND SELF-INSTRUCTIONS, students participate in the use of the strategy and the construction of the story. Once the story is completed, students identify things the teacher said that helped to: (1) get started, (2) write the story, and (3) evaluate the story. They record examples of statements (in their own words) that they will use to help themselves write. If students have good suggestions as to how to make the strategy more effective, the teacher and students collaborate on making any revisions at this time.

After students memorize the steps of the strategy, COLLABORATIVE PRACTICE begins. As they start practice, several tools for regulating the use of the strategy are further introduced, including goal setting, self-assessment, and self-recording.

Using stories written prior to the start of instruction as a baseline, students set goals for how many action words they will include in the story about to be composed. After the story is completed, the number of different action words used is counted and compared to the number established in the goal. They then record their performance on the graph developed earlier and note their success in attaining the goal. When goals are met, students are encouraged to set their next goals so that they do as well or better. Students continue to use the self-regulation procedures as they make the transfer to INDEPENDENT PERFORMANCE.

At first, some students will need help in setting realistic goals for their papers. We had one student who, although at that point using no action helpers in her writing, wanted to set a goal to include "28 action helpers" in her paper! Fortunately, the teacher was able to help her develop a more appropriate initial goal.

A final note to keep in mind is that some students become so enamored with setting and obtaining goals that the basic purpose — to write a good story — is forgotten. For instance, a student may use too many describing words or action helpers in a particular story. This may not be a concern initially, particularly if students are discovering a new type of word they rarely or never used before. One of our students, for example, included a 12-color rainbow in one story. If this continues to occur, however, students need to be reminded that words are only useful if they help to develop the story line.

What To Expect

After helping students learn to use this strategy, we found that their stories became longer and more entertaining. Not surprisingly, the number of different action verbs, adjectives, and adverbs included in their stories increased as well. Changes in the length of students' stories were not due solely to the use of more action verbs, adjectives, and adverbs. Students generated other types of story content as well.

The following stories were written by an elementary school student before, during, and after instruction in the strategy. This first story was written before strategy instruction.

Me and my son are leaving to fly a space shuttle. And some day, me and my son will hopefully fly one. My son says, "When he grows up, he going to fly one." When he finishes school, me and my wife are going to put him through school and let him learn how to fly. And when he starts to fly space ships, he will be able to buy his own house. Now that he's grow up, he will start flying in 3 months, and he said he, "I will love it a lot."

The following story was written after instruction in using the strategy with action words and action helpers. Note the overuse of adverbs in one sentence. This was not a concern at this point, since we believed overuse would diminish with further practice.

The Super Bowl Champions

One day in January, it was the Washington Redskins versus Miami Dolphins. Washington had the ball. First, Joe Theisman handed off to Riggins. Riggins ran ten yards and Joe went for a flea flicker and made an 80 yard catch and Joe threw fast to Charlie Brown and Brown caught it and made a touchdown. Miami had the ball. The quarterback fumbled wildly and recovered painfully and got up and got tackled crazily and kicked off anxiously and ran down the field quickly. Washington scored quite a bit but Miami did not. The last few seconds were happy. Redskins had the ball and let time run out and Washington Redskins were the world champions.

The third story was written after instruction on the use of the strategy with action words, action helpers, and describing words.

The Dog And His Food

One day this puppy was sitting on the porch, and these boys started throwing rocks at the puppy. And one hit the puppy, and the puppy sadly ran into the house. And the girl came downstairs and said, "I'm going to take the puppy for a walk." So she went and got the dog leash and took him for a walk. And when he was walking, she tripped and fell hard on a rock and cut her hand, and had to get 15 stitches on her hand. When she got home from the doctors, she went looking for the puppy. All day she looked, and then she saw him. She took him home and give him a bath, and after she gave him a bath she fed him a big bowl of dog food. And she was very happy that she found him.

Each of these stories was corrected for spelling, capitalization, and punctuation errors. As can be seen, the third story is more complete and richer than the first story. It contains more ideas, as well as more action words, action helpers, and describing words.

We found that students used the strategy when writing stories for other teachers, and continued to use it over the remainder of the school year. While they did not spontaneously use it following their summer vacation, they did remember the steps to the strategy and the definitions for the various vocabulary items. At this point, a booster session (discussing the strategy and reminding them to use it) was needed.

Extending The Strategy

The utility of a writing strategy depends not only on its effectiveness, but also on how well it can be adapted to other writing situations. While "brainstorming" action words and describing words may be useful prior to writing a story or a personal narrative, it is of little value when composing expository text such as an opinion essay. This strategy can be adapted so that it can be applied more widely by having students "brainstorm" any words or ideas that they think might be useful in writing their paper.

THE THREE-STEP STRATEGY WITH TREE AND SPACE: A PLANNING STRATEGY FOR GENERATING AND FRAMING WRITING CONTENT

Another means for helping students generate possible writing content is to make use of the basic structural characteristics that underlie various writing forms such as stories. For example, the "story grammar" strategy presented in the previous chapter encourages children to take advantage of their knowledge of the structure of common stories to generate and organize their own writing material. Prior to writing, students pose and answer seven questions, each involving the basic parts of a story. This helps them generate possible writing content for the story's setting and plot and provides a frame for organizing the information produced.

The concept of using discourse schema or frames to help students retrieve and organize possible writing content can be extended to genres other than stories. In this section, we present a general planning and writing strategy that is designed with this goal in mind. Students use the general strategy to guide the planning and writing process, while also applying a series of genre-specific prompts for generating, organizing, and evaluating possible writing content.

The Strategy

The "three-step" strategy consists of the following steps:

- THINK — WHO WILL READ THIS?
          WHY AM I WRITING THIS?
- PLAN WHAT TO SAY.
- WRITE AND SAY MORE.

The first step in the strategy encourages the writer to consider the purpose for completing the paper and the audience who will eventually read it. This helps the student set some general goals for what the paper will accomplish. During the second step, the student uses a series of genre-specific prompts (or a structural frame) to generate, organize, and evaluate possible writing content. The third step is a reminder to the student to use the plans already devised and to continue the process of planning while writing.

At the present time, two structural frames have been developed and field tested. The first frame is for the most fundamental form of an opinion essay and includes the following self-directed prompts:

- NOTE *TOPIC* SENTENCE.

- NOTE *REASONS*.

- *EXAMINE* REASONS — WILL MY READER BUY THIS?

- NOTE *ENDING*.

The mnemonic *TREE* is used to help students remember the key words in the frame (the words that are highlighted). When working on an opinion essay, therefore, step two (plan what to say) of the "three step strategy" becomes: *PLAN WHAT TO SAY USING TREE*.

One feature of the frame that merits special attention is that students are encouraged to make notes concerning their ideas for their essay. We had observed that some students would write their prewriting notes out as full sentences, converting the eventual writing task into a process of simply recopying their notes word-for-word. Furthermore, the strategy prompts the author to evaluate and reflect on the quality of supporting ideas before they are actually committed to paper.

The second structural frame that was developed is for story writing and includes the following prompts:

- NOTE *SETTING*.

- NOTE *PURPOSE*.

- NOTE *ACTION*.

- NOTE *CONCLUSION*.

- NOTE *EMOTIONS*.

To help students remember the key words for this structural frame, the mnemonic *SPACE* was used. Thus, the second step of the "three step" strategy becomes: *PLAN WHAT TO SAY USING SPACE*. The key words in the frame serve as a reminder to generate possible writing content concerning the setting (introduction of the main character, locale, and time of the story) as well as the plot of the story: what the main character strives to achieve (purpose); what is done to try and achieve the goal (action); the results of the action (conclusion); and the main character's reactions and feelings about various events in the story (emotions).

Teaching The Strategy

Students first learn to use the "three-step" strategy with a single writing genre. For instance, we first taught students to apply the strategy as they wrote opinion essays using the structural frame, TREE, to guide the planning process. Once students achieved this goal, they then practiced writing stories using the strategy and the structural frame, SPACE. The discussion on how to teach the strategy uses this sequence to illustrate the instructional process.

Prior to teaching the "three-step" strategy, teachers need to be sure that students have an audience for their papers. This will already be the case for students in a process approach to writing, since students are encouraged to share their writing both formally and informally with their classmates. If routines that promote student sharing are not in place, individual children can be paired with a peer reader with whom they share their written work. In fact, we recommend that students share their written work with an audience of their peers whenever possible, especially when learning to use any of the strategies presented in this book.

The first step in learning the strategy is to make sure that students are knowledgeable about the basic parts of a simple essay. During PRESKILL DEVELOPMENT, this goal is accomplished by using a small chart containing the mnemonic *TREE* and its four corresponding prompts. Each prompt is discussed as follows. NOTE *TOPIC* SENTENCE (prompt one), emphasizes the first part of an opinion essay that "tells what you believe." NOTE *REASONS* (prompt two), stresses another part of a "good opinion essay" that tells why you believe it or, in other words, gives good reasons to support your topic sentence. This is further stressed with the third prompt, *EXAMINE REASONS*, where each reason is evaluated in terms of its believability. NOTE *ENDING* (prompt four), features the final part of an opinion essay, a sentence that wraps up your argument. The teacher and students collaboratively generate a topic sentence (premise), reasons, and a conclusion for different essay topic suntil this can be done independently.

To help students remember the mnemonic and its underlying rationale, we used the following analogy:

"If you think about the parts of a *tree*, it will help you remember how the parts of a good essay are related. The Trunk is like your topic sentence. How are the trunk of a tree and your topic sentence similar? (Everything is connected to each of them.) The Roots are like your reasons. How are the roots of a tree like the reasons that support your topic sentence? (They support the trunk — just like reasons support the topic sentence.) It is also important to Examine the roots — just like you examine reasons. If they are strong, the trunk and the whole tree will be strong."

Basically, the instructional procedures for the initial conference, discussing and modeling the strategy and self-instructions, memorizing the strategy steps, and practicing how to use the strategy are identical to the methods outlined in Chapter Two and will not be reiterated here.

After students have mastered the use of the "three-step" strategy when writing opinion essays, the teacher and students discuss how the procedure can be used to respond to other types of classroom assignments. Students are told, "When you *PLAN WHAT TO SAY* you do not use *TREE* for other writing assignments; instead you think of possible things to say that make sense given your assignment." Students are then asked to identify some of the types of things they would *PLAN* for a story. At this point, the mnemonic *SPACE* is introduced on a small chart, and the meaning of each prompt is discussed and practiced. Students then practice using the "three-step strategy" with *SPACE* to write stories. Other types of writing assignments, such as book reviews, reports, and so on, can also be discussed and an appropriate structural frame developed.

What To Expect

After learning to use the "three-step" strategy to write essays, we found that students' papers were longer and they produced more convincing arguments. We also looked closely at the content that students included in their essays (see Appendix A for a description of our classification scheme). Prior to learning the strategy, less than 10% of students' papers contained all of the basic parts of an essay (premise, reasons, and conclusion), and almost 50% of their material was unrelated to their argument or served no discernible rhetorical purpose. Once they learned to use the strategy, students almost always included all of the basic parts of an essay (82% of the time) and the amount of nonfunctional text dropped to 15%. Students successfully used the strategy when writing for other teachers and continued to use it over time. Finally, students' confidence in their writing skills increased, and they recommended that the strategy be taught to other students.

The two essays presented below illustrate the type of change in students' performance that we found. These two essays were written by an elementary-age student with a severe learning problem.

BEFORE INSTRUCTION: No, because we went to for 180 and we need to have fun in the summer, and rest our brains before we start school again.

AFTER INSTRUCTION: I think they are necessary. If there were no rules, people would be doing whatever they want. Not listening to the teacher and eating gum, and screaming, and jumping on furniture. That is why we have rules. So the kids can obey them and we will have a nice school. So that is why I think rules are necessary.

Can you tell what question the student was trying to answer in the first essay? It was, "Should children go to school all year round?" With the second essay, you do not have to guess what the essay is written about. The author makes the purpose of the paper perfectly clear. It is also much more convincing and complete than the first essay. As before, both of these essays have been corrected for mechanical errors.

Similar changes were noted in students' skills at writing stories when using *SPACE* as part of the "three-step strategy." The quality of students' stories improved and they became longer and more complete in terms of including the basic parts of a story (the procedure we used to assess this is presented in Appendix B). The following two stories (corrected for mechanical errors), written by an elementary-age student, demonstrate the types of changes we found in children's writing.

BEFORE INSTRUCTION: The boy is running through the meadow where there is a lot of water, and trees, and high hills. He is running up and down to get to another side, and he must be happy or he would stop running.

AFTER INSTRUCTION: Once upon a time, long ago, an animal was shipped to a small country in Brazil. The men that lived there did not know what it was, and they went to their leader and told their leader what had happened. He came out, took the box to the top of a hill, because whatever was in the box, he did not want it to kill his men. The man got a net and went to open the box. The animal got out and bit him, and was running towards his men. The men did not want to get hurt, so they ran into their tent with fear, and the animal ran away. The leader got a bandage for his leg, and got the net and started after him. He finally caught the animal, and found out it was only a scared lion and carried him back. He told his men to come out and look. They walked out slow. The leader said, "Look, it is only a baby lion." They all pet it, and played with it, fed it, and they all became good friends with the lion. They were all happy, but pretty soon after that, the lion got bigger and wasn't friendly any more. So they let it go free. They were all upset, but they remembered all of the good times they had with the lion.

Extending The Strategy

There are several ways in which the "three-step strategy" can be extended. One is to develop additional structural frames that can be used for other literary tasks such as writing descriptions, directions, explanations, and so forth. In teaching students how to compare and contrast two different things when writing, for example, attention needs to be directed at clarifying what is being compared and contrasted, on what dimensions are they being weighed, and how are they alike and different. These basic components can be developed into an additional frame that students use to generate and organize possible writing content as they *PLAN WHAT TO SAY.*

The structural frames, TREE and SPACE, can also be modified so that they become more challenging. For instance, TREE was designed to help students write the simplest form of an opinion essay and is typically appropriate for use with elementary-age students. For students at the secondary level, a more complex frame is needed. Parts of an essay more relevant for older students might include: an introduction to the problem, the author's premise, reasons to support the premise, the counterposition, reasons to support or not support the counterposition, examples for clarifying specific points, and a conclusion.

We would like to emphasize that students will need practice applying any new or modified structural frame that is incorporated as an option when using the strategy. An elementary student who had been taught how to apply the "three-step" strategy when writing opinion essays made this abundantly clear to us. While she had not received any instruction in using *SPACE* as part of the strategy, she was familiar with the parts of a story and had discussed with the teacher that *TREE* is only used when writing opinion essays. Nonetheless, she tried to generate story content using *TREE.* As one might expect, she experienced a great deal of difficulty with framing the story and was not too happy with the results. Her teacher discussed planning using *SPACE* with her and she mastered this strategy easily and was much happier with the results.

PLANS: A PLANNING STRATEGY INVOLVING GOAL SETTING

In recent years, the composing process has frequently been characterized as a problem-solving task. In composing a report, for example, the writer must develop a personal representation of what the problem involves, including the identification of goals for writing and ways of achieving them. During or after writing, progress in achieving the goals is assessed. Depending upon the outcome of this evaluation, goals are redefined as necessary. These are the same kinds of processes—problem representation, goal setting, and the like—that people use when trying to solve a wide array of problems.

If writing is problem solving, then the writing tasks that children are assigned in school frequently can be described as ill-defined problems. This point can be illustrated by examining a typical school assignment: writing a paper for class. For this type of assignment, students often have vague or fuzzy notions as to what resources should be used to locate the needed information. They may be equally unsure of how many resources or references will be enough to complete the assignment successfully. Finally, when the paper is finished, they often have no way of determining or evaluating if the results of their arguments are compelling.

How can writers successfully deal with ill-defined writing assignments? One strategy that is helpful is to break the problem into several subproblems. A writing assignment, for instance, can be divided into several subproblems: (1) select topic, (2) access resources and generate notes, (3) organize notes, (4) write the paper, and (5) polish the paper by making final changes. By approaching the problem in this way, it becomes less overwhelming. A second means for dealing with an ill-defined problem is to complete a means-end analysis; figuring out what the final form of the paper will look like and determining the means by which the selected "ends" will be achieved. This helps to better define the writing assignment and make it more manageable.

The strategy examined next is structured around a means-end analysis — students set product goals for what their paper will accomplish and articulate how these goals will be obtained. In addition, the writing task is broken down into several related subproblems revolving around the goal-setting process.

The Strategy

The strategy consists of the following steps:

- DO <u>PLANS</u> - <u>P</u>ICK GOALS;

    <u>L</u>IST WAYS TO MEET GOALS;

    <u>A</u>ND MAKE

    <u>N</u>OTES,

SEQUENCE NOTES.

- WRITE AND SAY MORE.
- TEST GOALS.

The first part of the strategy involves developing a plan for what the paper will accomplish and say. This process is initiated by first selecting writing goals from a list developed by the teacher and students conjointly. The use of such a list is advantageous for several reasons. It reduces the complexity of the task by limiting the choice of goals to a manageable set of alternatives. In addition, teacher input into the development of the goals helps to insure that they are realistic (achievable by the student) and desirable (their accomplishment will improve the written product).

The goals included on the list can address a variety of different aspects. They might profitably concern:

- *General purpose of the paper* — "Write a paper that will be fun to read."
- *Completeness of the paper* — "Write a story that has all of the basic parts."
- *Length* — "Write a paper that is 120 words long."

  "Write a paper with ten sentences."

  "Write a paper with five paragraphs."
- *Specific attributes* — "Write a paper that has four reasons to support your premise."

  "Share with the reader four things about the main character."
- *Vocabulary* — "Write a story containing 15 describing words."
- *Sentence variety* — "Write a paper in which one-fourth of the sentences are either compound or complex.
- *Mechanics* — "Write a paper with no spelling errors."

These examples are not meant to be exhaustive, merely illustrative. Different goals can be included in each of the categories represented and other categories are possible as well. In developing goals, the guidelines outlined in the next chapter should be consulted: goals should be proximal, challenging, and specific. This is most easily achieved when the goal is a "product goal" — specifies in quantifiable terms what will be accomplished. A particular advantage of "product goals" is the amount to be accomplished which can be individualized for each student, and it is possible to determine if the goal has been mastered.

The astute reader will notice, however, that the first goal illustrated above ("Write a paper that will be fun to read") is not a product goal; this would be hard to quantify and equally difficult to determine if it has been accomplished. While such a goal is typically more vague than the other goals that are illustrated, it is no less important. The judicious inclusion of general writing goals coupled with more specific "product goals" provides a much more comprehensive and broader net for casting one's writing plan.

When planning their paper, students can select one or more goals from the list. Based on our experience, we would recommend that students' selections be limited to a maximum of three to four goals, and that at least one of these goals be a general writing goal. Some students may need to start with one or two goals, and may find product goals easier to work with initially.

As goals are picked, students record their selection (see Table 2 for a worksheet for completing the PLANS section of the strategy). A decision is then made as to how each of the selected goals will be achieved. Or, in other words, a plan of action for each goal is determined and is recorded on the PLANS worksheet.

Next, students make notes concerning what they will say in their paper. It is important to emphasize that the process of generating possible writing content and pursuing the "selected" goals should dovetail. Take, for instance, Jane — an elementary-age student — who decided to write a story that was "at least 120 words long." Her plan for accomplishing this goal included: (1) jotting down, prior to writing, as many ideas and words to use in her story as she could think of, and (2) periodically counting, as she composed, the number of words already written. As a result, the process of making notes and the first step of her plan complemented each other nicely.

The last step in completing PLANS is to sequence the notes. This is done by placing numbers by what will come first, second, third, and so forth. It is important that students understand that in the process of developing and sequencing notes they may return to any stage at any time. As they generate notes, thoughts concerning how a particular idea will fit in or where it will be placed will occur to them. Similarly, as notes are sequenced, they will think of additional "things to say."

This give-and-take process of generating and sequencing ideas also overlaps with the second major step of the strategy, WRITE AND SAY MORE. This prompt is a reminder for students not only to use their PLANS as they write, but to continue the process of generating

Table 3-2. Sample Worksheet for Completing "PLANS."

P̲ICK GOALS:

1.   2.   3.

L̲IST WAYS OF MEETING GOALS:

1.   2.   3.

A̲ND, MAKE
N̲OTES:

S̲EQUENCE NOTES:

and organizing their ideas. The planning that occurs as students write will modify and reshape the plans that were developed prior to writing.

The last step in the strategy is to *TEST GOALS*. Once the paper is completed, the student checks to see if the selected goals were achieved. A check is placed by each goal on the *PLANS* worksheet that was satisfactorily accomplished. If a goal was not obtained, the student considers how the paper can be revised to meet the objective. The new plan is then put into action.

Teaching The Strategy

The "plans" strategy can be used with a variety of writing assignments. Similar to our comments on the "three-step" strategy, we recommend that students initially learn to use it while working on a single type of writing assignment. Likewise, students will need practice in applying the strategy with each of the different goals targeted for instruction.

Our approach has been first to help students learn to apply the "plans" strategy while writing opinion essays, and then to extend the use of the strategy to other genres like story writing. As students learn to apply the strategy more broadly, the range of product goals they work on achieving can be broadened as well. Table 3 includes an example of a Goal Selection List that we developed with elementary-age students as they initially learned to use the strategy; there are three sets of goals involving the general purpose, completeness, and length of the paper.

The goals for general purpose and completeness are for writing opinion essays and stories, respectively. The goal for length was determined individually for each student (so as to be challenging and realistic) and can be adjusted periodically. We encourage students to work on three goals (one from each of the three areas) simultaneously while writing their papers.

Before proceeding further, we would like to indicate that there is nothing sacrosanct about starting with essays first or beginning with these specific goals. The starting point and the goals selected will depend upon the nature and characteristics of the students and the teacher's approach to writing. This particular setup, however, will be used to illustrate how we have taught this strategy.

During PRESKILL DEVELOPMENT, students learn to identify, define, and produce the basic parts of an opinion essay and story. They need to know this information in order to achieve the goals for

Table 3-3. Goal Selection Card for Teaching the "PLANS" Strategy

"PICK ONE GOAL FROM EACH SET."

PURPOSE:

_____Write a paper that convinces my friends that I am right.

_____Write a paper that is fun for my friends to read.

PARTS:

_____Write an essay that has all of the parts.

_____Write a paper that has all of the parts.

LENGTH:

_____Write a paper that is 60 words long.

_____Write a paper that is 80 words long.

_____Write a paper that is 100 words long.

_____Write a paper that is 120 words long.

Note: Length goals should be determined individually for each student; these numbers are illustrative only.

writing papers containing "all of the parts" (see Table 3). They also need to be exposed to several examples of papers that are "fun to read" and "convincing." This provides students with concrete illustrations of how other authors have fulfilled these goals.

As they learn to apply the strategy, using the instructional procedures outlined in the previous chapter, students often need considerable help in selecting goals, deciding how they will meet their "target" goals, establishing procedures for monitoring goal attainment, and revising their plans when a goal has not been achieved. These processes are repeatedly discussed and modeled, and students are encouraged to indicate what they would do as the strategy is demonstrated. For example, different plans for achieving the goal "to include all the parts" can be modeled on successive days. Likewise, student application of these processes needs to be monitored closely; they should be provided with hints and direct assistance whenever necessary. Once students can apply the strategy successfully to essay writing, its use in writing stories is modeled, followed by practice in applying it for this purpose.

What To Expect

The essays written by students who learned to use the "plans" strategy (following the methods presented above) became two to three times longer. They were also much more likely to include all of the basic parts in their essays—before instruction only one in five essays had all of the basic parts; after strategy instruction, nine out of ten papers were complete. Teachers indicated that the essays written after training were more convincing, while students noted that the strategy improved how they wrote and that it should be taught to other students. The students' level of commitment was further demonstrated by their continued use of the strategy over time.

The two essays presented below illustrate how the strategy improved the writing performance of a young student with learning problems. The mechanical errors in both essays have been corrected.

BEFORE INSTRUCTION: No, because it will be too hot. And you will miss fun things and going swimming.

AFTER INSTRUCTION: I think children should not be allowed to eat whatever they want. They will get fat and they might eat too much. Some of the calories are too high. They can get a toothache from sweets like cake, candy, and ice cream. That's why I believe that children should not be allowed to eat whatever they want.

The second essay is superior to the student's earlier attempt to write an essay on the advisability of children going to school in the summer. It contains a clearly stated premise, two good reasons to support the premise ("get fat" and "get a tooth-ache"), and a concluding sentence. The text related to getting "fat," however, could be improved through some simple resequencing.

The "plans" strategy had a similar impact on students' story writing. After receiving practice in using the strategy to write stories, students' papers became longer, more complete, and more entertaining.

Extending The Strategy

The most logical extension of the "plans" strategy is to the area of revising. Once students complete a first draft of a paper, goals for improving their written product could then be devloped presented. For a student writing a story, for instance, the following goals might be included on the Goal Selection List:

- "Include an additional character as part of the story."

- "Change the ending of the story to make it more exciting."

- "Change the time of the story to 150 years in the future."

- "Include a protagonist in the story who tries to stop the main character from achieving her or his goals."

- "Change the setting of your story to the planet Mars."

All of the goals on this list require students to restructure their story in some fundamental way, compelling students to make substantial changes in their papers. We would recommend that students only choose one or, at the most, two goals of this nature to work on at any given time.

Revising goals do not have to be this difficult; they could be as simple as "include an ending or tell how the main character feels at the end of the story." The type of revising goals selected should directly reflect students' needs and writing maturity.

Once a goal has been selected, the "plans" strategy would operate in much the same way as previously described. This can be illustrated with the first goal ("Include an additional character as part of the story") on the list above. After writing the goal on the *PLANS* worksheet, the student would consider who the new character would be and how she or he would fit into the story—recording plans for completing the goal and notes on the character. The pertinent sections of the paper would then be rewritten and the student would remember to say more, continuing the process of planning while revising. After making changes, the student would check to see if the goal was adequately attained and would make appropriate revisions if this were not the case.

SCAN: A REVISING STRATEGY

As a rule, students do very little revising. When they do revise, the changes made are usually confined to proofreading. Even college students frequently do little to revise the content of their papers! It is not surprising, therefore, that the revisions students make generally do not result in better writing.

Why are children's revisions so infrequent and insignificant? One reason is because they often have had little experience or help actually revising their papers. Another reason is that students view revising as a tedious task, requiring the recopying of material already developed. Third, some children's concepts of revising, and writing in general for that matter, focus on the mechanical demands of producing text. Fourth, changing the "substance" of what has been written is hard work and often difficult.

With these caveats in mind, we designed a strategy that students can use to revise opinion essays while working on a word processor. *WAIT*, don't put the book down or skip ahead to the next strategy! We realize that the strategy in this form cannot be used widely. Consequently, a modified and more general form of the strategy is presented as well.

The Strategy

The steps of the "SCAN" strategy are presented below:

- READ THE FIRST DRAFT OF YOUR ESSAY.
- FIND THE SENTENCE THAT TELLS WHAT YOU BELIEVE — IS IT CLEAR?
- ADD TWO MORE REASONS WHY YOU BELIEVE IT.
- *SCAN* EACH SENTENCE — DOES IT MAKE *SENSE*?

    IS IT *CONNECTED* TO MY BELIEF?

    CAN I *ADD* MORE?

    NOTE ERRORS.
- MAKE MY CHANGES ON THE COMPUTER.

The aim of the first step of the strategy, rereading the initial draft of the paper, is to reacquaint students with the substance of the paper. The second step encourages the writer to re-examine the sentence that contains the premise of the paper to make sure that it is clear and accurately reflects her or his belief. If it does not, then it is revised.

Next, students are invited to add at least two more reasons to support their topic sentence or premise. This step was included because many students write brief essays, failing to provide enough support to adequately defend their thesis. This step will be unnecessary for students who develop first drafts containing reasons that provide strong support for the premise.

The heart and namesake of the strategy is the fourth step. With the exception of the topic sentence which has already been evaluated, each sentence is "scanned" to see if it is: *(1) clear* — will the reader understand it; *(2) useful* — does it directly support the development of the argument; *(3) complete* — do more details need to be added to make the sentence better; and *(4) error free* — are there any mechanical errors that need to be corrected? For the fourth criterion, students are specifically directed to detect and correct any spelling, capitalization, or punctuation errors. To help them remember these four evaluation criteria, the mnemonic *SCAN* is used to remind students of the key words: **<u>S</u>ense, <u>C</u>onnected, <u>A</u>dd, and <u>N</u>ote errors**.

As students check the clarity of the topic sentence, add reasons, and *SCAN* sentences, changes are made on a hard copy (double spaced) of their paper generated by the computer. The next step of the strategy involves transferring all changes to the computer. Some more experienced computer users may be able to skip the process of making a hard copy of their paper, and make changes directly on the computer. In summary, the "SCAN" strategy encourages students to examine what they write in terms of clarity and cohesiveness, add material where necessary, and eliminate mechanical errors.

Teaching The Strategy

During PRESKILL DEVELOPMENT, students need to learn the basic parts of an essay, including how to define, identify, and generate each part. This is desirable for two reasons. First, successful use of the *SCAN* strategy is dependent on knowing the parts of an essay. For instance, students must know what a topic sentence is. Second, students use this knowledge to help them generate and organize writing content for their first draft, providing them with a richer paper on which to apply the strategy.

Since a computer is used as the writing stylus, students must also be reasonably adept at typing and computer operations, including saving files, centering titles, deleting and adding textual material, replacing material, and so forth. If these skills have not been developed, they must be taught or students should be taught a version of the strategy appropriate for paper and pencil instead (see next section).

As students master this strategy (using procedures discussed in the previous chapter), teachers need to pay special attention to helping them detect and correct problems in their text. When teachers model the strategy, for instance, the processes for locating text problems needs to be made clear: "As I say this sentence out loud, something doesn't sound right (doesn't make sense) — something is missing" or "The rule for starting a sentence is to use a capital; this word isn't capitalized." Similarly, teachers and students need to articulate how each problem can be fixed. During COLLABORA-TIVE PRACTICE, the teacher needs to give students feedback on the quality of the changes made as well as provide suggestive prompts when they are unable to locate a serious text problem or are having difficulty correcting one.

What To Expect

After learning the "SCAN" strategy, students we have worked with generally made anywhere from two to five times as many revisions. Almost three out of five of these revisions changed the text in some meaningful way; only one in three did so prior to strategy mastery. These changes in students' revising behavior were also associated with better writing: essays became longer, were more convincing, and generally contained fewer errors. Students continued not only to use the strategy over time, but became more confident in their ability to revise.

In providing an illustration of how the "SCAN" strategy affected students' essay writing, we will not include pre-instruction examples; the common approach to revising at this point was simply to try and correct mechanical errors and change individual words. The effects of instruction in the strategy can best be illustrated by examining the first and revised drafts of an essay written by an elementary-age student. This student basically used the strategy steps as a prompt to add more material. Only the final draft is presented, therefore, with the student's additions to the first draft highlighted. While the student did correct some mechanical errors between the first and second drafts, not all errors were corrected. This has been rectified in the example presented below.

I do not think children my age should be allowed to ride mini-bikes. I think this because it is very dangerous to ride a mini-bike and you could get *seriously* injured, like breaking a leg. Also, children of my age should not be driving, and *regular* bikes are cheaper to buy than mini-bikes and safer to ride. *If children my age got a mini-bike, they would probably ride it a lot, and mini-bikes make a lot of noise. That would distract people and make them very mad. Mini-bikes are almost just like motorcycles, so you need to do what motorcyclists do. You have to have a license, and I am not old enough for one.* And these are the reasons why I think that children of my age should not be allowed to ride mini-bikes.

The major changes made by the student were to *add additional detail* to two of the sentences and to *add two additional reasons.* Changes involving clarity and cohesiveness were not made, probably because they were not needed.

Teachers need to monitor how the strategy is used over time. One aspect to watch for is how well balanced students are in using it. One student we worked with stopped correcting mechanical errors altogether (although she was quite capable of doing so). We held a short discussion with her, explaining that we were pleased that she was making more substantive changes, but that she also needed to continue to correct spelling, capitalization, and punctuation errors. After the short "pep talk," the revisions she made included mechanics.

Extending The Strategy

In our wrap-up session with students, we discuss with them how the "SCAN" strategy can be used when writing with paper and pencil. Suggestions provided by students have included: add a step ("Write your first draft on every other line."), drop a step ("Read the first draft of your essay."), or modify a step ("Make my changes on the computer" changed to "Make changes as I rewrite my essay."). Although students modified the strategy in different ways, they were still able to use it successfully when making the transfer to paper and pencil; they continued to make the same types of changes they made when using the computer. It should be pointed out, however, that students preferred, as a rule, to compose and revise on the computer.

More important than extending the use of the strategy to paper and pencil is expanding its use to other writing tasks beyond the simple opinion essay. This can easily be done by eliminating the third step — "ADD TWO MORE REASONS WHY YOU BELIEVE IT" — and changing a single step in *SCAN* itself. By changing the "C" in "SCAN," the strategy can be used across a variety of writing tasks, as can be seen below.

•   <u>SCAN</u> EACH SENTENCE — DOES IT MAKE <u>SENSE</u>?

IS IT <u>CONNECTED</u> TO MY CENTRAL IDEA?

(Is this sentence important to developing my ideas?)

CAN I <u>ADD</u> MORE DETAIL?

<u>NOTE</u> ERRORS.

The Peer Revising Strategy:
A Revising Strategy Involving Peer Response

One of the most important aspects of learning to compose is the social conditions under which the writer operates. When the word "writing" is mentioned, we usually think of a single author working alone in an office or at home (as we primarily did in preparing this book). For young students, however, much of what they write is done in a classroom populated with other students and at least one adult. Because the social conditions of the classroom can have a profound effect on students' development as writers, it is important that teachers strive to create a supportive, pleasant, and nonthreatening environment in which the young writer can grow.

How can teachers create such an atmosphere? Among other things, teachers need to be accepting and encouraging of students' writing efforts. They also need to provide expert support through conferencing, written feedback, and the like. They should write in and out of class and share their writing with their students. In addition, teachers should try to develop a sense of community in their classrooms by promoting student sharing and facilitating collaboration among students. One promising means for promoting student sharing and collaboration is peer response — peers react and make suggestions concerning the substance of each others' work. This can be done either through written feedback or in person by an individual, small group, or the class as a whole. Peer response is also an effective means for improving students' revising skills, since it makes the audience an integral part of the process. By interacting with the audience, the writer comes to internalize their evaluation criteria and suggestions for revising.

The revising strategy presented in this section is centered around peer response — peers provide suggestions to each other on how to improve their first drafts using a specific strategy. We believe that the combination of peer response with strategy instruction is an especially powerful tactic. Strategy instruction provides students with an explicit framework or strategy for responding to a peer's writing. Peer response provides a meaningful social context for using the strategy; peers help each other understand how, why, and when the strategy is used.

The Strategy

The "peer revising" strategy includes the following two strategies:

REVISE

- *LISTEN* AND *READ* ALONG.

- *TELL* WHAT THE PAPER IS ABOUT AND WHAT YOU LIKED BEST.

- *READ* AND MAKE *NOTES* — IS EVERYTHING *CLEAR*? CAN ANY *DETAILS* BE ADDED?

- *DISCUSS* SUGGESTIONS WITH THE AUTHOR.

PROOFREAD

- *CHECK* YOUR PAPER AND CORRECT ERRORS.

- EXCHANGE PAPERS AND *CHECK* FOR ERRORS IN —

    SENTENCES

    CAPITALS

    PUNCTUATION

    SPELLING

- *DISCUSS* CORRECTIONS.

When using the peer revising strategy, each student is assigned a writing partner. After students complete the first drafts of their papers, they get together with their writing partners and each has a turn to respond to the substance of the other's paper. This is facilitated through the use of a structured format in which the paper is first read by the author while the peer reads along. The importance of "active" listening is stressed, and the read-along arrangement insures that the listener knows what is included in the paper; some students will not be able to read a paper unaided because of limited reading skills or because of errors in spelling, punctuation, etc.

After the paper is read, the peer tells the author what the paper is about and what she or he liked best. This helps to insure that the peer actually does listen and starts the peer response process off on a positive note. In telling what the paper is about, the peer is encouraged to note the main ideas or important parts. The students then exchange roles and repeat the process with the other paper.

Next, each student reads his peer's paper to himself, asking for help from his partner if a particular part of the paper cannot be read. As they read, each student asks two questions: "Is there anything that isn't clear?" and "Is there any place that more detail could be added?" If a part is hard to understand, a "?" is placed by it. Also, students are asked to make at least three suggestions for things that the writer could say more about; the suggestions are written directly on the paper.

The peers then get back together to discuss their recommendations with each other. Each student is encouraged to make suggestions for how the recommended changes can be carried out, and they question each other about anything that is not clear. The students then revise their paper using the peer's responses.

The second part of the strategy involves editing the papers for errors. Before giving the paper back to their partner, authors check their own paper, correcting any errors located. Students use the following checklist to help them complete this task:

- SENTENCES — READ EACH SENTENCE, IS IT COMPLETE?

- CAPITALS — ARE FIRST LETTERS OF EACH SENTENCE CAPITALIZED? ARE PROPER NOUNS CAPITALIZED?

- PUNCTUATION — IS THERE PUNCTUATION AT THE END OF THE SENTENCE?

- SPELLING — CIRCLE WORDS YOU ARE NOT SURE OF. CHECK SPELLING WITH YOUR WORD LIST, SPELLING CHECKER, OR DICTIONARY.

Students again exchange papers, and each independently uses the checklist to mark and correct any errors found. Finally, the students get back together and discuss any corrections that were made, and each makes a final draft of his/her paper.

Teaching The Strategy

In teaching students to use the "peer revising" strategy, we found it easier to have students do their composing at the computer. This eliminated the tedious and time-consuming recopying by hand that would otherwise occur. Additionally, students first learned to use peer response when revising for substance, followed by learning the strategy for proofreading.

Because the peer partners work together over a long period of time, great care must be taken as to how students are matched. They should be compatible and able to work together cooperatively without getting off-task too much. They should also be reasonably similar in their writing skills.

During PRESKILL DEVELOPMENT, the role of revision in the writing process needs to be discussed: "We revise and edit our papers before they are published in our writing book, posted on the writing board, or shared with a broader audience such as the principal, kids from other classes, or our parents." This places the strategy in the larger context of the full writing process.

During MODELING, we have found it to be especially beneficial to show students a videotape of two peers executing the strategy. Teachers who cannot make such a videotape could have two writers model the strategy for the whole class. The models will enjoy this, and students are more likely to commit to learning the strategy when they see their peers doing it.

When MODELING the "peer revising" strategy, it is important for teachers to emphasize that feedback and suggestions be given to "your partner" in a positive manner. As students are learning to apply the strategy during COLLABORATIVE PRACTICE, each pair needs to practice being both the writer and the editor. At first, especially with younger students, the teacher may need to provide the editor with considerable help in responding to the partner's paper, providing hints as to what portions of the paper are unclear or lacking in detail or even modeling the process again for the pair.

What To Expect

When using the "peer revising" strategy, we found that students not only revised more, but their writing became better. The effects of the strategy on students' revising and writing behavior are illustrated in these two drafts of a paper written by an elementary-age, learning disabled student with severe writing problems.

FIRST DRAFT. I wostto go to tapdanssing school wen I wos 4 or 5. I wos theonly boy there. Well thas not tow. I wosnt the only boy. There wos on othere boy. But the othere boy kewt. So there wos 5 or 6 grils and I boy me. So we pratck. And play came. And hers the inbersing port comes. we dans. And at the end ol the gril kist me.

SECOND DRAFT. I used to go to tapdancing school when I was 4 or 5. I was the only boy there. Well thas not true. I wasn't the only boy.

There was one other boy. But the other boy quit. So there was 16 girls and 1 boy me. So we practiced. And play came. And here's the interesting part. We danced. And at the end, all the gril kissed me.

Extending The Strategy

One way that the "peer revision" strategy can be extended is by gearing the complexity of the strategy upward or downward. For example, in the version of the "peer revising" strategy presented here, students asked questions about both clarity and detail. If this is too difficult, then the questions can center just on one of these attributes. Similarly, during the initial development of the strategy, our two colleagues — Barbara Stoddard and Charles MacArthur — had secondary students ask four questions about their partners' paper. These included:

PARTS? Does it have a good beginning, middle, or ending?

ORDER? Does the paper follow a logical sequence?

DETAILS? Where can more details be added?

CLARITY? Is there any part that is hard to understand?

When using this version of the strategy, secondary students made more revisions and wrote papers of higher quality. More importantly, their writing became better even when they were not receiving feedback from their partner.

Another useful modification of the "peer revision" strategy is to match specifically the revision questions to the type of paper being written. If students are learning to write fiction, for example, the questions could focus on the common parts of stories ("Do you need to know more about the main character?").

USING THE WRITING STRATEGIES IN TANDEM

To become effective writers, students need to learn a variety of writing strategies. Although teaching students a single strategy, one for preplanning for instance, may provide an immediate boost to performance, it will not be enough to carry them over the long run. This boost is analogous to the rush of energy that a tired kid experiences after eating a chocolate bar. The sugar from the candy allows him to get back out into the thick of things on the playground right now, but will not sustain his play for a very long time. In 20 minutes or so, he will be tired again. To keep up his energy, he needs a steady diet of good food.

In writing instruction, learning powerful strategies for planning and revising is an important part of that steady diet. Providing a quick fix, however, by teaching a single strategy will likely result in the same outcome that we noted in the tired kid above. The student will be able to get out there and use the strategy to respond more successfully to school writing assignments right away, assuming, of course, that the strategy taught is appropriate to the student and responsive to the types of assignments faced by the student. This initial boost will dissipate over time as the student's writing assignments become more difficult and deal with new topics or literary forms. Thus, instruction aimed at developing strategic behavior during writing must be a primary part of the composition program, not just a one-shot deal.

This developmental view has at least two instructional implications. One, teachers need to help students adapt and upscale the writing strategies they use so that they are responsive to their growth as writers and the changing demands of the curriculum across subjects and grades. Two, students need to develop a rich repertoire of strategies on which they can draw.

An obvious extension of our thesis is that the strategies presented in this book be taught in tandem. We are not recommending that each student be taught every strategy in this book. Instead, teachers should use the strategies presented as a framework for deciding what planning, revising, and management strategies should be taught to their students. One teacher, for example, might teach the students in her class the "three-step" strategy, the "peer editing" strategy, and specific self-regulation procedures such as goal setting (presented in the next chapter) — extending and modifying each of these procedures as necessary.

When selecting strategies, special attention needs to be paid to insuring that they mesh together smoothly. We also encourage teachers to look for creative ways to combine strategies. For example, the "story grammar" strategy and the strategy for "brainstorming" action and describing words can be merged together. Students could first jot down ideas for each story part using a story grammar frame and then generate possible action and describing words that would be used to develop that part of their story. Such a combination would increase the number of ideas students consider and help them reflect more on how each part will be developed.

Another example of how our strategies can be merged together is illustrated in the example below.

- THINK — WHO WILL READ THIS?

  WHAT KIND OF STORY DO I WANT TO WRITE?

- PLAN WHAT TO SAY USING *C-SPACE*.

  C — NOTE *CHARACTERS*

  S — NOTE *SETTING*

  P — NOTE *PROBLEM*

  A — NOTE *ACTION*

  C — NOTE *CONCLUSION*

  E — NOTE *EMOTION*

- TELL YOUR STORY TO A *PARTNER* AND *REVISE* YOUR PLAN.

  AUTHOR: TELL YOUR STORY USING YOUR NOTES.

  PARTNER: TELL WHAT YOU LIKED BEST.

  BOTH: DISCUSS IDEAS FOR MAKING IT BETTER.

  AUTHOR: MAKE NOTES ON YOUR PLAN SHEETS.

- WRITE AND SAY MORE.

Do you recognize the two strategies that are joined together here? They are slightly modified versions of the "three-step" and "peer editing" strategies. The *SPACE* mnemonic presented earlier in this chapter has been expanded to include "C—note characters."

With this strategy, students initially think about who the audience is and what kind of story they want to write — should it be funny, scary, realistic, sad, or exciting? Next, an initial plan for what the story will say is made using the structural frame, *C-SPACE*. Then the plan is shared with the student's writing partner — the writer acts as a storyteller using the notes that have been developed to create verbally the planned story. The partner first shares with the writer what she or he likes about the story and then they jointly discuss ways to make the story better. The structural frame, *C-SPACE*, is used to guide this process. For each story part, the pair discuss if and how it can be made better. They ask themselves, "Is it clear? Could it use more detail? Is it interesting?" Special attention is directed at making sure the problem in the story is clear and that it makes sense. The author makes notes on the original planning sheet about suggested changes and new ideas, and uses this revised scheme to write the story, continuing the process of planning while writing.

In teaching this strategy, students first learn the steps involving THINK, PLAN, WRITE AND SAY MORE. Once they become adept at generating a plan to guide their story writing, the "peer editing" component is introduced. At the present time, we are in the process of field testing this strategy. Our initial evaluation of the strategy has been positive.

OTHER STRATEGIES

The planning and revising strategies included in this chapter have covered such diverse activities as brainstorming, goal setting, peer response, and the use of textual frames to generate and organize content. There are also a number of other strategies for planning and revising that students will find useful. Two common strategies, not covered here, that school age children use when writing are visualization and semantic webbing. For example, when writing about a personal experience, it is often helpful to try to visualize the events as they occurred. With semantic webbing, the author uses a graphic "think sheet" to order main ideas and supporting details.

In addition to these strategies, teachers often decide to construct strategies of their own; strategies that are responsive to their particular students and situation. We would like to offer several suggestions here. First, the strategies that are taught to students must represent a "do-able" challenge, one that students can accomplish given adequate assistance and guidance from the teacher. Second, the critical parts or steps of the strategy must be based on a careful study of the composition tasks and the abilities and characteristics of the students who will use it. Once this is accomplished, teachers will find the following guidelines helpful.

1. The strategy should consist of a small enough number of steps or parts so that it can easily be remembered or mastered. The exact number of steps or parts will depend on the age and capabilities of the students and the difficulty level of the task. A good rule of thumb is that the strategy should include no more than three to six steps.

2. When devising each step, be brief and use the students' language. Remember that students have to understand and memorize the steps of the strategy. This will be easier for them if each step is simply stated and to the point.

3. Develop a mnemonic or labels for the steps. This provides a handle for remembering and talking about the basic parts of the

strategy. The mnemonic can be either a word, phrase, or sentence.

4. Design the strategy so that it can be scaled upward or downward. This is a practical recommendation meant to ensure that the strategy is adaptable. Thus, a strategy appropriately scaled to a student's initial level of ability can be developmentally enhanced as the student's writing skills mature. Likewise, a strategy that is initially too difficult can be simplified so that the student can use it successfully.

5. When possible, refine or extend strategies the student already uses. It is effective and efficient to take advantage of students' existing writing abilities when developing a strategy.

6. Involve students in the development, piloting, and evaluation of strategies as much as possible. (Suggestions for involving students in piloting and evaluation of strategies are presented in Chapter 6.)

TAP AND COUNT

We conclude this chapter by sharing a strategy developed by teachers in the Maryland public school system.[1] The concept for this strategy originated with a group of writing teachers involved in the Capital Area Writing Project. These teachers took the process writing approach into the schools, frequently working with reading teachers on developing an integrated curriculum framework. The reading teachers were working on integrating reading, writing, science, social studies, and so on, and on developing reading-writing links.

A common challenge faced by these teachers, from the upper elementary school through the high school, was helping students prepare for the Maryland Functional Writing Test. This test is designed to assess students' skills in writing narrative and expository compositions. The teachers wanted to develop a strategy that would be powerful and generalize beyond the functional test, and that could be developed, extended, and matured across the grade levels. They initially considered elements common across writing tasks. They determined that the need to identify and consider the writing task, the audience being addressed, and the purpose for writing applied to most writing demands. Thus, TAP was born:

T   task=
A   audience=
P   purpose=

The Count part of this strategy, however, varies depending upon the writing task. Count is used for prewriting and planning. The Count part of the strategy involves using a prewriting planning sheet, as seen in Figure 1. The planning sheet begins with a column for the topic sentence, followed by columns for the "Count." Each count represents a major idea to be developed. For example, when TAP and Count is used by older students to write a book report, there could be one chart for each chapter, or section, of the book. Each chart could then have Count columns representing how the chapter started, what happened in the middle, and how it ended. Or, if the book is a novel, there might be one chart for the beginning, one for the middle, and one for the end of the story. Younger students, on the other hand, might have one chart for a book, with Counts for the parts of the story.

In each Count column students learn to make notes about the basic idea they want to develop, and elaboration. Some students use these columns to write out, revise, and organize incomplete sentences and notes, while other students find it easier to write out full sentences and then revise and order the sentences.

Versions of TAP and Count have sprung up for many writing tasks, and have been developed by both teachers and students. TAP and Count has been used for writing book reports, friendly letters, business letters, responses to the Advanced Placement History Test, stories, and answers to multiple forms of writing prompts on the Functional Writing Test. Both teachers and students have found this strategy helpful for several years now. Teachers have reported that with the aid of TAP and Count, more students have been able to pass the Functional Writing Test. The same observation has been made regarding the Advanced Placement Test.

Teachers and students have given several reasons why TAP and

Figure 3-1. TAP and Count Planning Sheet

T=	A=	P=

		Count	
Topic Sentence	1	2	3

Count is so useful. Both teachers and students we have talked with have noted that TAP and Count helps with organizing thoughts and with creating a structure for writing. A single Count frequently becomes a paragraph in the composition, thus also helping with style. Students have noted that the chart makes writing easier because they can work on one idea at a time, and go back and forth among their ideas easily as they plan. They have also noted that TAP and Count makes writing easier because it "helps your memory." Having the chart means less things to try and remember at one time, allowing students to concentrate on the content and meaning of their writing. Several students have mentioned to us that with the strategy and the chart they are able to write longer papers, because they "put as much detail as possible on the chart." Finally, teachers have noted that TAP and Count helps students to comprehend the writing task—to have a clear idea of what they are writing, for whom, and why.

Andy: An Illustration

One teacher we have worked with began by teaching her fourth and fifth grade students with learning disabilities the story grammar strategy discussed in Chapter 2. She felt that her students did so well with that strategy that they were ready for TAP and Count. The students agreed. She began use of TAP and Count with writing prompts similar to those the students would encounter on the fifth grade writing test.

The teacher had the students answer a question for each part of TAP and Count, filling in their notes on a prewriting planning sheet similar to the one seen in Figure 1. Thus, in this instance, TAP and Count stood for:

T(ask): What do I have to do?

A(udience): Who do I have to write to?

P(urpose): Why do I have to write?

Count:

Topic Sentence

1. How did it begin?

2. What happened in the middle?

3. How did it end?

The students learned to use the TAP and Count strategy through the same basic instructional process (self-regulated strategy development, discussed in Chapter 2) they had used to learn the story grammar strategy. However, as both the teacher and students noted, their knowledge of the story grammar strategy and experiences in learning it made learning TAP and Count easier and faster. The students mentioned many advantages of both strategies. They and their teacher had created "6 Writing Steps" for the use of the TAP and Count strategy (note the similarities to the steps involved in the use of the story grammar strategy):

1. Look at the prompt and read it.

2. Let your mind be free.

3. Write down the strategy (TAP and Count) reminder.

4. Write down ideas for each part.

5. Fill in your chart.

6. Write your story, use good parts and make sense.

Andy, one of the students in this class, described his attitudes toward writing before strategy instruction as quite negative. As he put it, before he started learning writing strategies, he just "didn't do much writing." He noted that he usually got very frustrated with writing and just quit. His teacher described him as a "non-writer" before strategy instruction began.

We visited Andy's classroom one day while he and several other students were using the TAP and Count strategy to respond independently to the following writing prompt:

"Suppose your teacher asks you to write about a special event you once celebrated. This event may have happened recently or long ago. Write a paragraph or more for your teacher telling about the special event you celebrated. Before you begin writing, think about the special event. Think about how the celebration began, what happened as it continued, and how it ended. Now, write a paragraph or more for your teacher, telling about the special event you celebrated." In response to this prompt, Andy wrote the following during the class period:

The District Run-Off

This event started in 1988 at the District Run-Off. My Pinewood Derby car had been chosen for best looking car in my pack. Because of this, I got to enter my car in the District Run-Off. The District Run-Off was a week from that day but it seemed like two months because I was so excited.

When it was finally the day of the District Run-Off, my Dad woke me up at 6:00 in the morning. I was very tired but I forced myself to get out of bed because I was so excited. When I got out of bed I got my uniform on and I ate a good breakfast. Then I got my Pinewood Derby car and got in our car and we were on our way.

When we got there, there was a big crowd there. I turned in my car at the best looking stage and I was very nervous, but we found a seat. First they showed the cars for the fastest cars. Then near the end they showed the cars for the best looking. After they showed all the cars the judges decided the best looking cars. When they were finished it was almost time to go home.

My car hadn't been chosen for any of the best looking so we went home, but I was still proud because I got a chance to go to the District Run-Off.

After Andy had written this story and read it to the group, we asked him what was different since he had learned the two writing strategies. His response, "I know how to do it!" When we asked him if he had changed the strategies he had learned in any way, his response was, "Seriously, I don't know how to write a letter, I can't write a letter. So I've changed my letters into stories." Andy had found an exciting, and creative, way to generalize the strategies he had learned. Finally, Andy mentioned that his favorite statement to himself while writing was now, "I can do this if I try." The use of self-speech, as well as other self-regulation procedures that have helped Andy and many other students develop as writers, is discussed further in the next chapter.

END NOTE

We would like to thank the teachers who have shared TAP and Count with us. In particular, Sam Oliver provided many details about the strategy and its history, and was responsible for many of the adaptations of TAP and Count to different writing genres, including friendly and business letters and the Advanced Placement Test. Arlene Bennof modified TAP and Count for story writing, as well as for responding to the fifth grade writing test, and invited us to visit her classroom as students were learning this strategy. We also would like especially to thank Phillip, Kevin, and Andy for sharing their writing with us.

REFERENCES TO STUDIES IN WHICH
THE STRATEGIES WERE FIELD TESTED

Graham, S., & Harris K.R. (1989). A components analysis of cognitive strategy instruction: Effects on learning disabled students' compositions and self-efficacy. *Journal of Educational Psychology, 81*, 353-361.

Graham, S., & Harris K.R. (1989). Improving learning disabled students' skills at composing essays: Self-instructional strategy training. *Exceptional Children, 56*, 201-214.

Graham, S., & MacArthur, C. (1988). Improving learning disabled students' skills at revising essays produced on a word processor: Self-instructional strategy training. *Journal of Special Education, 22*, 133-152.

Graham, S., MacArthur, C., Schwartz, S., & Voth, T. (in press). Improving LD students' compositions using a strategy involving product and process goal-setting. *Exceptional Children.*

Harris, K.R., & Graham, S. (1985). Improving learning disabled students' composition skills: Self-control strategy training. *Learning Disability Quarterly, 8*, 27-36.

MacArthur, C., Schwartz, S., & Graham, S. (1991). Effects of a reciprocal peer revision strategy in a special education classroom. *Learning Disabilities Research and Practice, 6*, 201-210.

MacArthur, C., & Stoddard, B. (1990). Teaching LD students to revise: A peer editor strategy. Paper presented at the Annual Meeting of the American Educational Research Association, Boston, MA.

Sawyer, R.J., Graham, S., & Harris, K.R. (1992). Direct teaching, strategy instruction, and strategy instruction with explicit self-regulation: Effects on learning disabled student' compositions and self-efficacy. Manuscript submitted for publication.

CHAPTER FOUR

Strategies for Self-Regulation: Managing the Writing Process

When working on his seminal book, *Origin of the Species*, Charles Darwin became concerned because he was not able to stabilize the amount of work completed each day. His wife, Emma, suggested that he use his "Sandwalk Technique": before starting to write each day, decide how many pages should be completed, represent each with a pebble in a pile on the sandwalk outside his study, and kick one away each time a page is completed until the pebbles are gone. Darwin was able to make this work for him by making a slight modification. Each time he proved a point and provided a footnote to buttress it, he would walk around the sandwalk and kick a pebble away from his self-assigned pile.

Hemingway was also known to establish a daily goal for the amount of material he planned to write. If the goal was met, one way he rewarded himself was with a night on the town. When the tally was not achieved, he stayed home that evening.

These two anecdotes illustrate that even professional writers who have developed a considerable repertoire of knowledge and skills find it helpful to use strategies to regulate the composing process and maximize writing performance. In the two examples, the authors used a variety of self-regulation strategies to direct their writing behavior. These included goal setting, self-monitoring (including self-assessment and self-recording of performance), and self-reinforcement contingent on performance. In this chapter, we examine how these same procedures, as well as self-instructions, can be used to manage and improve the writing of school-aged children.

While these four basic self-regulation abilities are discussed separately in this chapter, in fact they all are closely interrelated. For example, we will see that self-reinforcement involves some elements of both goal-setting and self-evaluation.

SELF-INSTRUCTIONS

Mature writers commonly talk to themselves as they write. They hold a running dialogue with themselves, making comments about where they are, what needs to be done next, why some idea does or does not work at this point, how they will phrase a certain idea, what a great job they are doing, and so forth. While this dialogue is occasionally out loud (overt), it is neither intended nor adapted for communication with others. Most of this private or self-speech serves the general cognitive functions of orienting, organizing, and structuring the author's behavior. In effect, writers tell themselves what to do while they write.

The Development Of Self-Speech

Self-speech develops naturally among most children. When do children learn to use private or self-speech to regulate their behavior? Some researchers believe that even toddlers' early egocentric speech is a primitive form of self-regulation. Young children's speech to themselves during play or other activities is capable of not just accompanying action but of capturing and directing it. Young children are also able to use self-verbalizations for emotional release. These verbalizations, however, are typically involuntary and also occur during action.

How do young children learn to use private or self-speech to regulate their behavior? Interactions with parents and significant others provide a powerful base for the development of self-regulation in young children. Initially, the adult takes major responsibility for planning, directing, and evaluating during activities; a great deal of this process is modeled for and shared with the child as the adult either talks to the child or thinks out loud in front of the child. Gradually, the child develops the ability to use self-speech to plan, direct, and evaluate her or his own activities.

At first, young children's self-speech occurs out loud. In fact, the amount of overt self-speech used by children typically increases until the age of 6 or 7. Overt self-speech then decreases and self-speech becomes primarily covert or internal by the age of 8 to 10, as children's cognitive capabilities increase and they become aware that it is not socially acceptable to talk out loud to yourself in front of others (children with developmental delays or learning problems may continue to use quite a bit of overt self-speech even beyond the age of 10). Over time, covert self-speech becomes quite abbreviated and condensed, and may be seen as one step removed from "pure thought."

What are Self-Instructions?

When students are taught to use self-speech to regulate their own behavior, we call these self-verbalizations self-instructions. Typically, we teach students to use self-instructions that are aimed at helping them comprehend the writing task, produce effective and efficient writing strategies, and to use these strategies to monitor and mediate their writing behavior.

In writing and other academic areas in the classroom, self-instructions perform numerous functions. They can: (a) direct the student's attention to relevant events, stimuli, or aspects of a problem; (b) help the student to interrupt or control an automatic or impulsive response (in other words, to stop and think); (c) assist the student in generating and selecting alternative courses of action; (d) help focus the student's thinking; (e) aid memory for steps and procedures; (f) assist the student to perform a sequence of actions or steps; (g) help the student deal with anxiety, frustration, or other forms of arousal, and (h) stipulate criteria for success. In addition, self-instructions have important motivational aspects. Self-instructions can enhance positive task orientation, elicit an achievement set, reinforce and help maintain task-relevant behaviors (helping the student spend more time constructively engaged in the task), and provide ways of coping with failure and self-reinforcing success.

An example. The ways in which self-speech aids self-regulation of goal-directed behavior either in writing or other academic areas can be illustrated with an example familiar to all teachers. Consider the self-speech that may occur while a teacher prepares a lesson. Our hypothetical teacher is experienced, and thus little to no self-speech is required as she prepares to work. Almost automatically, she gets her plan book and related books and materials, sharpens a couple of pencils, and then gets situated in her preferred work environment. As she begins to work, she engages in several cognitive processes, including self-speech, imagining, anticipating, and self-monitoring. Her internal dialogue begins something like this: "What is it that I want them to understand?" As she works, her internal dialogue primarily consists of abbreviated messages to herself, consisting of just a few words or short phrases, such as "They should be able to..." "I`Il try this." "Last year... " or "I can use...". Routine planning steps are frequently taken care of with little or even no internal dialogue.

When a problem is encountered, however, she begins to think more in full sentences, asking herself: "How am I going to get this across?" As she begins to work out an idea, she finds herself uttering out loud, "No, no, that isn't going to work." Evaluating her students' anticipated reactions, she determines, "This is too hard, I've got to find a better way to help them get it, especially Pat." As she works out the problem, self-evaluation and self-reinforcement messages include, "I've got it" ... "This is going to be a good lesson." Before the final kinks and steps are worked out, however, she reaches a point where she would rather be doing something (anything, she thinks) else. Coping messages enable her to stay on-task and meet the goal she set for herself when she began; she says to herself, "I can do this if I try... If I get this done, I can relax later and won't have to worry about it...I can enjoy the weekend." These self-statements, and imagining what she will be doing when this is done, are effective again as they frequently have been in the past, and she settles down and finishes. The final product is a lesson plan she feels good about and looks forward to implementing and evaluating next week.

Mature writers use private or self-speech to perform all of the functions just illustrated in this example. Young writers can be taught to use self-instructions for these same purposes. In addition, self-instructions can help students engage and monitor writing strategies for planning and revising (see Chapter 2).

We now turn to the types and levels of self-instructions that students can learn to use, procedures for helping students learn to self-instruct effectively, and a discussion of practical guidelines and issues in the use of self-instructions in writing and the classroom in general.

Types and Levels of Self-Instructions

We typically teach young writers to use *up to* six different types of self-instructions. Each of these six types can be developed at two levels. Depending on the students and the task at hand, teachers may choose to help students learn to use all of the types and levels of self-instructions, or some subset. Additional types not on our list can also be developed by students or teachers in response to specific needs.

The Six Types

The first type of self-instructions is *problem definition*. This type of statement allows students to determine the nature of the writing task and what it is they need to do. Self-questioning, followed by statement of answers or possible solutions, is a common part of problem definition. For example, a student might say to himself, "What is it I need to do here? I want to write a good story; I need to remember that good stories are fun to read and have seven parts."

The second type of self-instruction is labeled *focusing of attention and planning*. As the label indicates, these statements help students to focus on the task at hand and generate a plan (determine the strategies or procedures to be used). For instance, a student might say to herself, "First I need to remember my writing strategy for story writing," and, when necessary, "Take my time, let my mind be free."

Strategy self-instructions are the third type that can be developed. These statements allow students to engage and implement writing or self-regulation strategies (such as the goal-setting or self-monitoring strategies). Thus, a student might say, "First I will write down my story strategy reminder. The first step in the story writing strategy is ...," and "In order to set my goals for this story I first need to ..."

The fourth type of self- instruction includes *self-evaluating and error-correcting* statements. This type of self-instruction assists students in evaluating performance and catching and correcting errors. For instance, a student might say to herself, "Am I following my writing steps — let me check each one." or, "I forgot the setting, I'll need to add that in."

The fifth type of self-instruction is termed *coping and self-control*. These statements help students to subsume difficulties or failures encountered and to deal with forms of arousal such as anger, frustration, stress, and anxiety. These statements are highly individualized and responsive to the characteristics and needs of individual students. They can be aimed at personal characteristics, such as impulsivity, a low tolerance for frustration, learned helplessness, and so on. For instance, one of our students found that he worried quite a lot about writing and decided to say to himself, "Don't worry, worry doesn't help." He found this to be very helpful. Other students we have worked with have used statements such as, "I need to take my time and look carefully at each step," or "It's ok if I get it wrong, I can erase."

Finally, *self-reinforcement* is the sixth type of self-instruction. Students choose self-statements used to reward themselves for progress made, coping with problems, persistence, and the quality of their

Table 4-I. Illustrations of the Six Basic Types of Self-Instructions

Problem Definition
Sizing up the nature and demands of the task:
   "What is it I have to do here?"
   "What am I up to?"
   "What is my first step?"
   "I want to write a convincing essay."

Focusing of Attention and Planning
Focusing on the task at hand and generating a plan:
   "I have to concentrate, be careful...think of the steps."
   "To do this right I have to make a plan."
   "First I need to... then..."

Strategy
Engaging and implementing writing or self-regulating strategies:
   "First I will write down my essay writing reminder."
   "The first step in writing an essay is..."
   "My goals for this essay are...; I will self-record on..."

Self-Evaluating and Error Correcting
Evaluating performance, catching and correcting errors:
   "Have I used all of my story parts - let me check."
   "Oops, I missed one; that's ok, I can revise."
   "Am I following my plan?"

Coping and Self-Control
Subsuming difficulties or failures and dealing with forms of arousal:
   "Don't worry, worry doesn't help."
   "It's ok to feel a little anxious, a little anxiety can help."
   "I'm not going to get mad, mad makes me do bad."
   "I can handle this."
   "I need to go slow and take my time."

Self-Reinforcement
Providing reward:
   "I'm getting better at this."
   "I like this ending."
   "Wait `til my teacher reads this!"
   "Hurray - I'm done!"

writing product. For example, a student might say to herself, "Good,I'm doing fine," "I'm getting there," or "I like my story." Further illustrations of these self-instructions can be found in Table 1.

It is not necessary to worry too much about what category a self-statement fits into; rather, teachers should focus on helping students decide what kinds of self-instructions they could profit from using and helping them create self-instructions in their own words. For instance, one group of students with whom we worked wanted to have some self-statements to help with creative thinking for story writing. After a group discussion with the teacher, they devised their own personal statements, including, "Let my mind be free," Let my mind play," "Take my time — good thoughts will come to me," "Think of new words for old ideas," and "Think of an idea no one else would ever think of." It may not be clear which of the six categories these statements fit into; they could be considered strategy, planning, or self-control statements. It really doesn't matter.

We don't use the labels for self-instructions given in this book with young students, either. Rather, we work with them to develop self-statements in categories such as "Things to help me be creative, think free," "Things to get me started" (problem definition and focusing and planning self-instructions typically go here), "Things to say while I work" (focusing and planning, strategy, self-evaluating and error-correcting, coping and self-control, and self-reinforcement type statements could all go here), and "Things to say when I'm done" (evaluation and error-correcting, and self-reinforcement type statements typically fit here).

When students are first learning to use self-instructions, it may be best to start with only one type or even only one self- instruction that fits a particular need for the individual student. Otherwise, students might be overwhelmed with lots of different types of statements to try and remember to use. Most of the students with whom we have worked, including students with severe learning and writing problems, have caught onto self-instructions quickly and have then been ready to expand their repertoire.

The Two Levels

In addition to different types, self-instructions can also be developed at two different levels: task-approach and task-specific. *Task-approach self-instructions* are global self-management or task-management statements that can be used across a wide variety of tasks

(writing, reading, social situations, etc.)

Task-approach statements can have a powerful impact on behavior and performance and may help students generalize self-regulated behavior to other tasks and settings. For instance, the statement, "What is it I have to do here?" is a problem definition statement at the task-approach level. This statement can be used by students to help cue themselves to stop and determine the nature of the task on a wide variety of school assignments.

On the other hand, the self-statement, "I need to write a story that has all seven parts," is a problem definition statement at the task-specific level. Task-specific self-instructions are most relevant to the task at hand, and typically have little use with other tasks. They are, however, very powerful in terms of promoting successful performance on the immediate task.

There is little research available as to which of the six types of self-instructions, at what level, are most important. We believe students should develop the types and levels of self-instructions that fit their needs and interests. Once again, it is not necessary to worry too much about what level a statement falls into. Rather, teachers should help students develop powerful self-instructions that they can use across writing (and other academic areas) as well as self-instructions that are helpful to specific types of writing assignments, like writing a story.

Teaching Students To Use Self-Instructions

The Little Professor. One of our favorite illustrations of the importance and usefulness of teaching self-instructions comes from a first-grade classroom the first author visited in Indiana several years ago. She was doing research on the types of self-statements kindergartners and first graders with and without learning problems used during problem solving. The children were left alone in one part of a room with a puzzle to put together; a hidden microphone picked up their spontaneous self-speech as they worked. She had rigged the puzzle so that it could not be solved; a center piece had been professionally recut and painted so that it looked like it went with the puzzle but could not be fitted in (lest you think us cruel, all students were told after they quit trying to work the puzzle that she had goofed and given them a piece that went with another puzzle — they were then given the correct piece and were able to or helped to finish the puzzle!).

As predicted, the normally achieving children were typically using several strategies to work on the puzzle, accompanied by quite a bit of out-loud, task-relevant, helpful self-speech (remember, before the age of 8-1O, young children frequently use quite a bit of overt self-speech as they work). The young children who were experiencing learning problems, on the other hand, were quite consistently failing to attack the puzzle in any strategic way (picking up pieces to try at random, and so on) and were using predominantly off-task and negative self-statements. For example, one little girl talked at length to herself about what she would do at Brownies (a visit with the teacher revealed that Brownies was not for four days!), while one little boy sang a song about going on a trip to Idaho. Most of these students also frequently made negative statements to themselves about both puzzles and their abilities, such as "I hate puzzles," or "I'm no good at puzzles." In addition, most of these students quit trying the puzzle after just a minute or two and never even reached the rigged piece (this puzzle, without the rigged piece, could be done by most 5-year-olds).

Toward the end of the study, in walked an adorable young boy who was experiencing learning problems in the first grade. His black shoes shined, he had a crew cut, and he wore a jacket, bowtie, and glasses (it must have been school picture day). After a few warm up activities, the first author left him alone with the puzzle board and pieces and went to do some paperwork at the other end of the room. At first it looked as if his performance would be consistent with that of the other students with learning problems; in fact, he appeared to be quickly getting quite frustrated and hadn't gotten even one piece in. Imagine the first author's delight (and consternation in terms of how his performance was going to affect the data) when all of a sudden this young boy pushed himself back from the table, carefully folded his hands in his lap, took a deep breath, and in a sing-song voice said, "I'm not going to get mad, mad makes me do bad." This young boy, instantly dubbed "The Little Professor," used this single self-instruction several times while he worked on the puzzle, and it always helped him to calm down and try again. He was able to complete more of the pieces and had a longer working time than any of the other students with learning problems.

Of course, the first author couldn't wait to talk to his teacher — just how had it come about that he was able to spontaneously use this self-instruction so appropriately and so well—and in a new situation? The teacher was a young woman who had never heard of self-speech, self-instructions, or cognitive strategy instruction. As she put it, she simply believed that the things we say to ourselves have a great deal of power over our behavior, performance, and feelings about ourselves. Thus, during weekly class meetings, the students helped each other to identify one thing they needed to work on and to develop a helpful self-statement. The teacher initially reminded each student to use her or his statement when appropriate and modeled its use for the student. She reduced assistance and cues to use the self-statement as a student became able to use it independently. When a student had been successful with a particular self-statement for some time, he or she could choose a new thing to work on.

At a recent class meeting, The Little Professor had identified getting mad when he was working as something that kept him from doing his best work. He and the class had worked out the statement, and the teacher had suggested pushing back and taking a deep breath. He was now using this self-statement and relaxation strategy frequently and independently in the classroom. Obviously, he was able to generalize it as well. Imagine what a wonderful present this teacher was giving her students; at the end of the year each student would have a repertoire of powerful, individual self-instructions to carry on with them. Imagine the power of such an approach over the school years, across teachers and classrooms. Basically, that is what cognitive strategy instruction is all about.

It is worth noting that later in the puzzle solving study students with and without learning problems participated in a 20-30-minute strategy instruction session. Each student watched and discussed a 6-minute videotape of a 9-year-old boy who self-instructed out loud while completing a similar puzzle. He used several puzzle-solving strategies and all six types of self-instructions we've described. Each student was then left alone with the rigged puzzle. The students both with and without learning problems performed significantly better on the puzzle and used more strategies and task-relevant self-speech than did the students who had not received strategy instruction. The differences, however, were most marked among the students with learning problems; on some measures these students actually outperformed the students who were not experiencing learning problems. This study and the story of The Little Professor help to illustrate both how powerful self-instructions can be and how easily they can be taught.

General guidelines

Teaching students to self-instruct is typically done in much the same way as it was done by The Little Professor's teacher. The importance of what we say to ourselves and how the things we say can help or hurt us is discussed with an individual student or group of students. Sometimes teachers begin teaching students how to use self-instructions by modeling how they use them in a certain situation or on a particular task. Then each student is assisted in developing a meaningful self-instruction or set of self-instructions in her or his own words. Modeling of the use of the self-instruction(s) by the teacher or a peer is critical in helping students learn to use the statement(s) effectively. Students are then prompted and assisted in the use of the statements as necessary. Modeling, prompts, and assistance are gradually reduced as students master use of the self-instructions. Evaluation of the efficiency and effectiveness of the self-instructions should be done regularly and collaboratively. Once a student is using the self-instructions effectively, the teacher and student may discuss and implement generalization of their use in other appropriate situations. If a student appears to stop using the self-instructions over time, the teacher can once again provide modeling and assistance as needed.

Students can be taught to use one or more self-instructions alone, or the use of self-instructions can be taught in combination with one or more of the other self-regulation procedures we discuss in this chapter (goal-setting, self-monitoring, and self-reinforcement). The more severe a writer's problems are, the more complex instruction becomes. When students need to learn both self-regulation skills and planning and revising strategies, we recommend the use of full-blown self-regulation strategy development procedures.

Practical considerations

It is very important that individual students develop self-instructions in their own words. Self-instructions are typically not effective unless they are matched to the student's verbal style and language level. Thus, while the teacher may initially model a self-instruction or set of self-instructions, each student should then decide upon the wording of his or her own self-instructions. If a student chooses to use a statement identical to one the teacher has modeled, the teacher must be sure that this statement is meaningful to and appropriate for the student. It will do a student little good to use a self-instruction that he or she does not truly understand or feel comfortable with. It is not a problem if students abbreviate or modify a self-instruction once they have begun using it, as long as the self-instruction continues to fulfill its purpose. Teachers should be alert, however, to changes in self-instructions that decrease their effectiveness or subvert their purpose.

The use of self-instructions also should not be taught in a mechanical, rote-learning manner. Rather, the teacher should be enthusiastic and model the use of self-instructions with appropriate phrasing and inflection. Students should use self-instructions in the same way. It is important that the model (whether teacher or peer) have a positive, favorable relationship with the student. Remember, also, that the student is not merely the passive recipient of the self-instructions and behaviors modeled, but rather plays an active, collaborative role in the design, implementation, and evaluation of self-instructions.

Modeling of self-instructions can be done effectively on an impromptu basis, during writing activities, games, discussions, instruction, and everyday occurrences as appropriate. Although live models—the teacher, another student, or another adult—are typically preferable, other alternatives have been used successfully. For example, cartoon characters and drawings have been used to help students learn self-instructions aimed at slowing down and thinking before acting or writing. A written list of statements, tape-recorded statements, and videotaped models have also been used successfully.

In fact, some teachers have improved student performance by having the target student model for other students (same age or younger); this gives the target student a special incentive to learn to use the self-instructions and provides a very positive experience for the student. One of the teachers we have worked with is building a videotape library by having students who are experiencing problems in math master self-instructions and strategies for math tasks (long division, problem solving, etc.). Once a student is proficient at self-instructing through a task, he or she is videotaped doing so at the board and this tape can be used to begin strategy instruction for the next student who needs help on the same task.

Correspondence between saying and doing is also important when self-instructions are used. Merely saying the right things, or doing the action or task and then saying the self-instruction, is usually ineffective. Students may need some assistance in developing a close correspondence between self-instructions and the writing behaviors or cognitions they are meant to control. If a student has a great deal of difficulty achieving correspondence between saying and doing, then the self-instruction may be too difficult or inappropriate in some way.

Some students, particularly older students, may resist the use of overt verbalizations because they find talking out loud to themselves to be embarrassing or inappropriate for their age or situation. Students should not be forced to use overt verbalizations, or for that matter any form of self-instructions, against their will. Several researchers have noted that students respond more favorably to learning to use self-instructions when they are asked to "think out loud" rather than to "talk out loud to yourself," and when it is explained to them from the beginning that overt use of self-instructions is temporary. Covert, internal use of self-instructions is the goal, and some students can progress quite quickly from modeled, overt, induced use of self-instructions to covert self-speech. It may help to explain to students that you need to hear them use the self-instructions out loud initially just long enough to be sure that they are using them appropriately and that they are effective.

Students who continue to resist the use of overt self-instructions might be allowed to practice in a private area, to whisper, or to speak into a microphone (older students find this to be meaningfully different from talking out loud to themselves!). If these options are not acceptable, the student might choose to write her or his self-instructions down and read them when appropriate. However, this may not be as effective as using the self-instructions overtly at first.

Finally, overt verbalizations may interfere with behaviors that are timed, occur quickly, require reflexive reactions, or involve complex processing. For example, many young children find complex self-instructions cumbersome and difficult to use when they are learning to print. Simple statements, on the other hand, can be helpful. We have rarely found self-instructions to interfere with performance when they are appropriate to the students' needs and characteristics (including language and cognitive capabilities) and to the task at hand. Both the teacher and student should carefully evaluate self-instructions to be sure that they are indeed appropriate and are not interfering with performance.

GOAL SETTING

A second self-regulation procedure that we have helped young writers learn to use is goal setting. Goal setting procedures provide a useful heuristic for attacking many writing tasks. For instance, in writing a term paper for a biology class, a student might first decide to write a paper on birds that will be ten pages long, concentrate on three different types of birds, and receive at least a "B" grade. A good writer will operationalize these criteria by developing a manageable plan that specifies a sequence of activities for attaining the goals: "I'll get three books on birds to read, decide which birds to study, watch these birds myself at the park on Saturday and Sunday afternoon, determine what information from the books and my personal observations should go in the paper, and count the number of pages produced as I write."

As the student works on the writing project, progress in achieving these goals, as well as the plan used to achieve the goals, will need to be assessed periodically. It may be necessary to redefine the plans or a particular goal: "I identified three birds, but I only saw two of them in the park. I have a lot more information than I thought I would, so my paper will compare how these two birds' behaviors are similar and different."

We do not wish to imply that the process of goal setting is always this neat nor that the only meaningful types of goals in writing concern what the end product will look like. Sometimes writers start off with vague notions and intentions that become sharpened while in the process of gathering information or attempting to express ideas in writing. Similarly, as writers become more engaged and familiar with the problem, previously unconsidered goals may be created. Writers also create goals to deal with immediate problems such as, "I need to write a good sentence to tie these two ideas together."

Nevertheless, heuristics such as the one described above provide several advantages for young writers. They supply a means for making a complex problem like writing a term paper more manageable. By defining what the paper will look like or accomplish, writers provide greater structure and focus on what they want to accomplish, while at the same time limiting the possible solutions that can be used to complete the exercise. In addition, developing an operational plan that breaks the writing problem down into a series of related subproblems and provides a specific sequence of activities for how to proceed makes the writing task more structured and less overwhelming.

In examining the use of goal setting, we first consider how goal setting acts to affect students' performance and what factors need to be attended to if the power of goal setting is to be maximized. This is followed by exploring ways in which goal setting can be used as part of the writing process.

The Dimensions of Goal Setting

Across a wide variety of human endeavors, goal setting has been shown to be an effective tool for improving performance on tasks ranging from the amount of weight truck drivers carry in each load to the amount of material read by students. Why is goal setting so effective?

One reason why goals are such good regulators of human action is that they enhance motivation. At the most fundamental level, goals direct attention and action to what needs to be done. Moreover, a personal commitment to achieve a goal provides an incentive to mobilize effort. The anticipated satisfaction in attaining the goal leads one to further sustain efforts over time until the goal is accomplished or exceeded. Goals can also motivate a person to develop or create a plan of action for their attainment.

In addition to heightening motivation, goals also serve an informational function by allowing an individual to compare his or her present performance against the standard embodied in the goal. For example, if an individual observes that adequate progress is being made in obtaining a desired goal, this is likely to amplify one's personal sense of efficacy. This, in turn, can further increase motivation for accomplishing the goal. Thus, goal setting provides an incentive to perform and promotes pride in accomplishment. For students, this can lead to increased engagement while working on a task, more rapid learning, and a heightened sense of personal accomplishment.

Properties of Goals

Goals exert their effects through their properties. The properties that appear to be especially critical to the successful use of goal setting in writing and other academic areas are specificity, difficulty, and proximity.

Specificity. Goals that supply a specific and clear standard of achievement ("Write a paper citing 20 references.") result in better performance than goals that are vague ("Do some referencing.") or when no goals are provided at all. Why are specific goals superior? Because they provide a clear indication of what is required and it is easier both to plan and to gauge progress if the standard is explicitly stated.

Difficulty. Goal difficulty refers to how hard or challenging a goal is for a particular person. Goals that are challenging lead to better performance than goals that are easy. If a goal can be achieved with little or no effort, there is little incentive to mobilize effort or resources. On the other hand, if the goal is difficult to begin with, effort and resources must be mobilized to achieve it. A qualification is in order, however. Harder goals lead to better performance only when one has made a commitment to obtain the goal and has the capability to achieve the goal.

Proximity. Goals also differ in their proximity. Goals that are proximal are close at hand and can be completed quickly, ("Write three pages in your journal today."). In contrast, goals that are distal are to be completed farther into the future, ("Write 30 pages in your journal in the next two weeks."). Proximal goals lead to higher levels of performance than distal goals. The problem with distal goals is that they may be too far removed in time to stimulate students to mobilize their resources here and now. For example, we are all familiar with students who have a five-week period in which to complete a term paper, but wait until a couple of days before it is due to start. Proximal goals yield more opportunities for determining how things are going (at least on a daily basis for the journal writing example) and provide more occasions for inducing an individual to take action.

To summarize, goals that are specific and challenging are preferable to no goals or goals that are specific and easy. Furthermore, goals that can be accomplished in the very near future are preferable to long-term goals.

Other Considerations

Feedback. The success of the goal-setting process also depends on a number of other factors. An especially important axiom is that knowledge of how one is doing in achieving the desired goal is necessary for goals to improve performance. This can easily be illustrated by considering the efforts of a friend of ours who was attempting to lose weight. His initial attempts involved setting a goal to lose ten pounds over a one- to two-month period. His plan for achieving this goal involved cutting out between-meal snacks and eliminating lunch.

Unfortunately, his efforts at monitoring his progress were sporadic. Instead of weighing himself regularly, he would go for weeks without checking his progress, or only check the day after he had done some strenuous exercise (you probably know someone like this). It should come as no surprise that he was often disappointed when he got on the scale, and he indicated that he would often backslide on his eating plan except on the days he actually weighed himself. The story has a happy ending, however. He took a friend's suggestion and began weighing himself first thing every morning. This daily feedback on how he was doing provided him with the incentive to stick to his plan.

As this example illustrates, feedback or knowledge of how one is doing is necessary if an individual is to track his or her progress and attain a desired goal. Feedback can influence performance by causing one to expend the amount of effort still required to achieve the goal, try new strategies if success is lagging, reset easy goals to more challenging ones, and establish new goals once an earlier goal has been accomplished. Timely and frequent feedback is especially helpful because it encourages evaluation and control of one's own behavior on an ongoing basis.

For school-aged children, feedback on how they are doing in attaining goals can be obtained from either the teacher or peers, or through self-assessment. In the long run, it is more beneficial if students are encouraged and assisted (when necessary) to self-monitor their own goal attainment. Students will be much more successful in doing this when goals are stated specifically and are easy to measure.

Who sets the goal. Another influential consideration in goal setting involves the student's role in setting the goal. Goals can be either assigned by the teacher, determined by the student, or participative. With participative goals, the teacher and the student both contribute to goal development and/or selection. For example, the student may select one or more goals to achieve from a list of goals developed conjointly by the teacher and the student.

We recommend that participative goals be emphasized, at least initially, for several reasons. It has been our experience that many beginning writers have difficulty setting reasonable and realistic goals for themselves. We are reminded of a young elementary student we were working with who wanted to set a goal to include 100 action words in his next story even though his compositions were usually about 50 words long. His teacher was able to bring this expectation back down from the stratosphere by first discussing the feasibility of this goal, and then suggesting a range of more reasonable goals for the student to consider.

Participative goals also offer specific advantages to students who have writing problems. Because these students often have little confidence in their ability, the process of developing their own goals can be quite a struggle. A possible solution would be for teachers to simply tell these students what they want them to achieve. However, we believe it makes more sense to make students participants in the process, since this helps lead to perceptions of ownership and a greater level of commitment to achieve the goals. The teachers' eventual aim, however, should be that all students will determine their own goals. Participative goal setting provides a useful bridge for promoting this objective.

When helping students design and select goals, it is important to keep in mind that goals beyond their capabilities will not lead to improved performance. No matter how committed students are to achieving a goal, exerting more effort will not result in success if the goal is too hard. Thus, teachers need to be sensitive to helping students select goals that they can attain or at least approach attaining. Teachers can extend students' capacity for achieving many goals, however, by teaching them appropriate strategies for attaining the goal.

Goal acceptance and commitment. At this point it should be obvious that a person's acceptance of a goal and her or his commitment to attain it are essential to the success of the goal-setting process. How, then, can teachers foster students' goal acceptance and commitment?

- Being supportive is vital.

- Teachers should listen to students' opinions about the goals, encourage questions, and ask students what they plan to do to meet the goals.

- Goals are also more likely to be accepted if they are seen as valuable. While some goals are intrinsically valuable to students, many academic and writing goals are not. One way that teachers can make a writing goal more attractive is to link its accomplishment to a reward. In part, this is the role that grades are supposed to serve, but often do not. If rewards are offered, they must be desirable to students. That does not mean that they have to be expensive or fancy. They can be as simple as 15 minutes of free time on the computer.

- Before using such rewards, however, we would recommend that teachers first try the self-reinforcement procedures presented later in this chapter.

- Finally, nothing succeeds like success. Goals are more likely to be accepted by students if they have a high expectation for achieving them. If students have a history of success in meeting their goals, then they are more likely to be confident and try to achieve even higher goals.

Goal Setting During the Writing Conference

Conferencing between student and teacher is a common practice in writing instruction. Conferences may occur before, during, or after writing. Conferences are used for a wide range of purposes, including checking on students' plans or intentions, seeing how things are going, giving feedback, providing assistance as needed, or helping students reflect on what they have done. Within the process approach to writing, conferencing is one of the most prominent means by which teachers help students extend control over the writing process.

Writing conferences provide an excellent medium for incorporating a goal-setting heuristic into the writing program. Assisting students in clarifying their plans and intentions is one of the functions that conferencing is supposed to fulfill. Furthermore, by taking advantage of an existing instructional mechanism such as conferencing, teachers will find the implementation of goal-setting procedures easier to achieve.

A Goal-Setting Heuristic: SCHEME

How can goal setting be integrated into the writing conference? A goal-setting heuristic we have used as part of the conferencing process provides an illustration of how this can be done. This goal-setting strategy, referred to as *SCHEME*, has six steps:

- Skill Check
- Choose Goals
- Hatch Plans
- Execute Plans
- Monitor Results
- Edit

Skill check. The purpose of the first step, *Skill Check*, is to complete an inventory of how the student is presently doing. This provides the information necessary to make informed decisions regarding the selection of goals. There are two basic arrangements for determining a student's present level of performance. One, the student can complete an inventory independently. For instance, a recently completed paper or a current work in progress might be examined to note specifically what has and has not been done. Teachers can facilitate such a self-check by developing with students a checklist highlighting specific items that need to be considered. For example, when writing directions, the checklist might include determining if the following basic elements were included: reason for directions, starting point, destination (both location and description), distance, mode of transportation, estimated amount of travel time, complete description of route, reference to landmarks, map, and an account of possible complications that might arise.

A second way of completing the Skill Check is for the teacher and the student to work together. Direct assistance from the teacher might include any of the following: a backup check to confirm the validity of the student's own assessment, a collaboration where student and teacher jointly complete the assessment, or a presentation of the teacher's assessment of the student's current performance.

Choose goals. The second step in *SCHEME* is to *Choose Goals.* Our description of this step is consistent with our earlier suggestion that goals be either self-determined or participative. At least initially, the participative approach should be used until students become familiar with goal setting and how to construct goals. This can be facilitated through a three-step process.

1. First, students select goals to complete from a list of goals constructed by their teacher.

2. Next, the teacher and students work together to construct goals for completing specific writing assignments.

3. Finally, students are encouraged to construct their own goals, receiving assistance only when necessary.

Once students can construct their own goals, then "C" in *SCHEME* can be changed to "Construct Goals." An important point to keep in mind is that goals should be based on the data from the Skills Check and should be specific, challenging, and proximal.

Hatch plans. In the third step, *Hatch Plans*, the strategies or action plans the student will put into operation to meet each goal are specified. For example, the student would specify what steps will be taken to insure that the written directions have all of the elements mentioned previously. In addition to specifying "how" the goal will be met, it can also be helpful to establish when and where the plan will be put into operation as well as who will be available to provide assistance. Thus, a student might indicate that he will write the directions Wednesday night at home and ask his mother to read and follow the directions the next day to make sure they are complete.

We recommend that students be encouraged to write their plans down. This not only provides students with a reminder of what they intended to do, but gives teachers a window for examining students' plans. This is important because the processes they plan to put into play may be incomplete or flawed in some fundamental way. In some instances, students may need to develop a plan of action collaboratively with the teacher.

Execute plans and monitor results. Although the fourth step of *SCHEME*, *Execute Plans*, is self-explanatory, the fifth step, *Monitor Results*, bears some discussion. *Monitor Results* refers to assessing both goal attainment and the plan used to achieve the goal. In our earlier illustration, the student would be encouraged to assess whether or not the directions were adequate and contained all of the basic elements. Moreover, he would be urged to consider whether or not the plan was used as intended and to evaluate its success.

Edit. If a student is unsuccessful in meeting the goal, actions to remedy this situation are put into effect during the final step, *Edit*. For instance, if the student failed to include directional markers and a description of the destination, a decision could be made to rewrite the directions. In addition, the student might decide to establish an additional goal at this point (make the directions amusing) and start the process rolling all over again.

An example. To make the process more concrete, we would like to share an example of one way *SCHEME* can be used to help students plan their compositions. We illustrate this process with two teachers: one working with a group of younger students on story writing (including a student named Greg), and one working with an older group of students on essay writing (including Leah).

The first step in the process was to collect stories or essays the students had written recently. The teachers first looked for the meaning or message communicated in each paper. They then examined the completed papers, noting specific strengths and weaknesses. They noted whether or not the papers had a clear purpose, were complete, and logically organized. In addition, papers were examined in terms of length, sentence and vocabulary variety, and amount of elaboration.

Based on this assessment, Greg's and Leah's teachers developed a list of goals responsive to the needs of the students in their respective classes. For stories, goals involved the number of action and describing words included and the completeness of the story. For essays, goals centered around providing reasons in support of the premise, making statements expressing an opposite side, and providing examples or elaborations on reasons.

The teachers then conducted a mini-lesson with these groups in order to insure that all of the students were familiar with the concepts embodied in the goals. In Greg's group, the students and teacher together defined and identified action words, describing words, and the basic parts of a story: characters, place, time, a starting event, the characters' goals and reactions, action to achieve the goals, and resolution or ending. Throughout the discussion, the role of each in promoting story quality was emphasized. Similarly, in Leah's class, the students and teacher discussed basic parts of an essay, including premise, reasons to support premise, reasons on the other side, examples or elaborations on reasons, and conclusion. Students in both classes made a chart containing all the parts of either a story or an essay to keep in their writing folder.

Once the mini-lesson was completed, the first step of *SCHEME* was activated. Teachers discussed with students their performance on a particular story or essay written previously. For example, Greg's teacher told him that she liked his story, noting things she especially enjoyed and that she was pleased with how hard he had worked. Together they found that his story had seven action words, three describing words, and contained all but three of the story parts: a starter event (What happened to make the prince want to flee his kingdom?), the characters' reactions (How did the prince feel?) and an ending. Each of these attributes was visually highlighted — describing and action words were circled and story parts underlined. The teacher and Greg then discussed how he could improve his story writing by concentrating more effort on these areas.

At this point the teachers held another mini-lesson with their classes. They described the goal-setting heuristic and discussed how this would help students improve their writing, as well as when and where it could be used. Students were told that they would each meet individually with the teacher to help develop their goals. Greg, for example, developed goals involving having all the parts of a story, and a minimum of ten action words and eight describing words. The teachers concluded the lesson by modeling how to use the *SCHEME* heuristic, "thinking aloud," as they went and involving students in the process as much as possible.

Over the next several weeks, the students and their teachers established a standard routine for writing. When students were ready to start a new story or essay, they would confer with the teacher. The teacher started each conference by asking students what they planned to write about, or by helping students brainstorm about topics. Next, students chose at least two goals to work on from their list. Students were encouraged to vary their goal selection and goals were occasionally upgraded or developed for new writing targets. For each goal selected, students were asked to write down or hatch a plan. While students were in the process of writing their papers and executing their goals, the teachers checked in periodically to offer advice and provide assistance.

When a paper was completed, another conference was held and the teacher encouraged the student to monitor or assess success in obtaining the goals and using the plans. The teacher verified the student's assessment and perhaps provided additional performance feedback on goal areas not selected. If a goal was not met, the student was encouraged to edit the paper or to make the necessary modifications to ensure success. Finally, throughout the individual conferences, teachers were friendly and helpful, encouraging students to ask questions and make suggestions.

For Leah and several other students in her class, the teachers had to provide additional support. Leah's goals were to write an essay in which she provided four reasons to support her premise, refuted two reasons on the other side, and provided four clarifying examples. She was at a loss as to how to go about accomplishing any of these goals. During their first conference, therefore, her teacher modeled a simple organizing strategy for her to use. The steps of the strategy included deciding on a premise, reading selected relevant materials, brainstorming (for either reasons, examples, or counter-reasons), and having another member of the class evaluate the believability of each item generated. With support from her teacher, Leah became adept at applying the strategy by the time she wrote her third essay.

This example using *SCHEME* is responsive to the guidelines for effective goal setting we established earlier. Goals were specific, challenging, and proximal. They were also individually determined, increasing the likelihood they were achievable. When goals appeared to be too difficult, however, teachers provided students with additional support. Students' acceptance and commitment to achieving goals were also championed, since the process was participative and conducted in a supportive environment. Finally, students were aware of how they were doing as they evaluated their own efforts and received feedback from their teachers.

The use of goal setting in writing can be extended in a number of different ways. For instance, goals can be set for revising a paper rather than planning a paper. Or, instead of setting goals for improving a specific aspect of students' written products, goals can be aimed at increasing productivity. For example, goals can be set for amount of pages written in a personal journal or number of written homework assignments completed. While students are learning a planning or revising strategy, they can also be encouraged to set a daily goal to use the strategy.

SELF-MONITORING

Self-monitoring occurs when a student determines whether or not, or how often or for how long, a specific behavior has occurred, and then self-records this in some way. Thus, self-monitoring contains two elements: self-assessment and self-recording. While self-assessment can be done without self-recording, most students do better when they use the two together. Many students have also told us that self-recording is their favorite self-regulation procedure. For these reasons, both self-assessment and self-recording are examined together in this section. It should be kept in mind that once students are proficient at using self-regulation procedures to manage the writing process, they may primarily choose to use self-assessment alone. Self-recording, however, necessarily involves self-assessment and should not be used alone.

Self-monitoring can help writers activate the processes involved in writing and improve what they write. Self- monitoring can occur before students begin writing (during goal setting and planning, for example), while they write, or after they have a completed draft. In order for self-monitoring to be effective, both the self-assessment and self-recording procedures must be easy for students to use independently, minimally obtrusive or laborious, appropriate for the students' needs and the task at hand, and enjoyable. With these guidelines in mind, we first discuss self-assessment and self-recording, then present the steps we follow in teaching students to self-monitor, and finally discuss some practical guidelines and issues in the use of self-monitoring in the classroom.

Self-Assessment

Self-assessment involves determining whether or not, how often, or for how long an event or behavior has occurred. For example, students might ask themselves whether all of the parts of a good story were used. Or, they might determine how many words were written in the story, or how long they spent writing.

At least initially, it is preferable for students and the teacher to decide collaboratively what will be self-assessed. Because self-assessment prompts students to compare their own performance to standards for acceptable performance, the teacher and students should also determine criteria for acceptable performance. It is easy to see how goal setting and self-monitoring work well together. If goals have been set, then either the objective or the processes used to reach the objective can be self-assessed, and the criteria for acceptable performance are stated in the goal. A student who has set a goal to have ten good describing words and five good action words in her story would count the number of action and describing words in her completed draft and compare these numbers to ten and five, respectively.

Because the goal is for students to self-assess independently, the self-assessment procedures must be within the students' capabilities, or means to support independent self-assessment must be found. A teacher we worked with recently taught her students to self-monitor the number of times they wrote their spelling words in a 15-minute practice period each day; the students then entered their counts on their individual graphs. Happily, these students found the self-monitoring procedures to be quite motivating and increased their daily number of spelling practices from approximately 20 to approximately 75; on several days some students' practice counts exceeded 120! (Our research indicates that self-monitoring of spelling practice meaningfully improved both initial mastery of spelling words and maintenance of correct spelling.) However, the teacher quickly realized that one young lady could not count above 50; she supplied this student with paper which was numbered in columns and the student was able to resume independent self-assessment and self-recording. Finally, it is also important to note that the writing task or process chosen for self-monitoring should be meaningful to the student and within the student's capabilities.

Self-assessment can focus on either the writing process or product. Although students can self-assess more than one aspect of their writing, it is best to begin with just one target for self-assessment. Additional targets for self-assessment can be added or addressed later and should be determined collaboratively by conferencing with the student.

Writing products that may be self-assessed include fluency (number of words written or number of paragraphs written), number of good story parts included, number of elaborations given, and so on. Students might also assess the amount of time spent writing. Although fluency may not be the most important goal in writing, helping students learn to write and say more is an important aspect of writing instruction. As college professors, we frequently find that undergraduate and even graduate students turn pale when required to write papers longer than 3-5 typed pages! As they learn to write more, students learn to extend content, elaborate on concepts, provide detail, and reduce anxiety regarding length. Setting goals to write and say more, as well as self-monitoring these goals, can be helpful in this process. It is interesting to note that many famous authors, such as Ernest Hemingway, Anthony Trollope, Arnold Bennett, Irving Wallace, and Charles Darwin, routinely set daily writing goals for themselves and kept detailed records of the number of pages or words written. As Irving Wallace put it, these writers did not write only when touched by mystic inspiration, but rather invested their work with professionalism and used self-regulation strategies to help maintain their productivity.

Length should not, however, be the ultimate criteria for self-assessment. We know a high school teacher who tells his students that topical papers due every 2-3 weeks must be a minimum of 15 pages long (handwritten) to be turned in. After that, length has nothing to do with the grade received. Grading has to do with clearly specified aspects of both content and style. This seems an appropriate way, with high school students, of making length one aspect of their composition goals.

Aspects of the writing process can also be self-assessed, including issues related to the task or topic, structuring the environment to facilitate writing, planning, revising, maintaining motivation, seeking assistance, etc. An illustrative list of process targets for self-assessment is provided in Table 2.

With some elementary school students who were learning to use more action words, action helpers, and describing words to improve their writing, we used an after-writing questionnaire to enable students to self-assess several aspects of both the writing process and product. The students answered *yes* or *no* to the questions listed in Table 3, and discussed their answers with the teacher. In addition, students counted the number of target words (describing words, for example) in their stories and entered their counts on their individual graphs.

Table 4-2. Writing Process Checklist

DIRECTIONS: Place a check by each action that you did while writing this paper.

Time and Place
____ I set up a schedule for when I would work on the paper.
____ I found a quiet place to work.
____ I got started working right away.
____ I kept track of how much time I spent working on this paper.
____ I always had the materials ready that I needed each time.
____ I sat down to work.

Understanding The Task
____ I read or listened to the teacher's directions carefully.
____ I asked the teacher to explain any part of the assignment that was unclear to me.
____ I restated what I was supposed to do in my own words.

Planning
____ I thought about who would read my paper.
____ I thought about what I wanted my paper to accomplish.
____ I started planning my paper before I actually started writing it.
____ I used a strategy to help me plan my paper.

Seeking And Organizing Information
____ I tried to remember everything I already knew about this topic before starting to write.
____ I got all the information I needed before starting to write.
____ I organized all of the information I had gathered before starting to write.

Writing
____ I thought about what I wanted my paper to accomplish as I wrote.
____ I thought about the reader as I wrote.
____ I continued to develop my plans as I wrote.
____ I made revisions in my paper as I wrote.

Revising
____ I revised the first draft of my paper.
____ I checked to make sure that the reader would understand everything I had to say.
____ I checked to make sure that my goals for the paper were accomplished.
____ I made my paper better by adding, dropping, changing, or rearranging parts of my paper.
____ I corrected errors of spelling, capitalization, punctuation, and the like.
____ I used a strategy to help me revise.
____ I reread my paper before turning it in.

Seeking Assistance
____ I asked other students for help when I needed it.
____ I asked my teacher(s) for help when I needed it.
____ I asked my parents or other people for help when I needed it.

Motivation
____ I told myself I was doing a good job while I was working on the paper.
____ I rewarded myself when I finished the paper.

Table 4-3. Describing Words Story Questionnaire

Please answer each question below. Circle your answer.

When you wrote your story,

1. Did you look at the picture and write down good describing words? YES NO

2. Did you let your mind think free? YES NO

3. Did you like the words you thought of? YES NO

4. Did you remember your goal—to use more good describing words than last time? YES NO

5. Did you think of a good story idea? YES NO

6. Did your story make sense and use good describing words? YES NO

7. Did you read your story and then fix it? YES NO

8. Did you take your time? YES NO

9. Did you remember to use everything you know about writing stories to help you while you wrote? YES NO

10. Did you tell yourself that you did a good job? YES NO

Self-Recording

Self-recording involves having students record whether or not, how often, or for how long the selected behavior or event occurs. Thus, in the case of describing words, circling *yes* or *no* on the questionnaire or entering the number of words on a graph constitutes self-recording. Individual graphs or charts are frequently used for self-recording, as they present a picture of the student's performance over time and allow the student to see improvement. This visual record of improvement has proven to be highly motivating to the majority of writers with whom we have worked. It is also interesting that even when students were not taught to set goals, the use of graphs stimulated them to do so—typically to equal or surpass their graph from the previous day. Sample self-recording graphs are provided in Figures 1, 2, and 3.

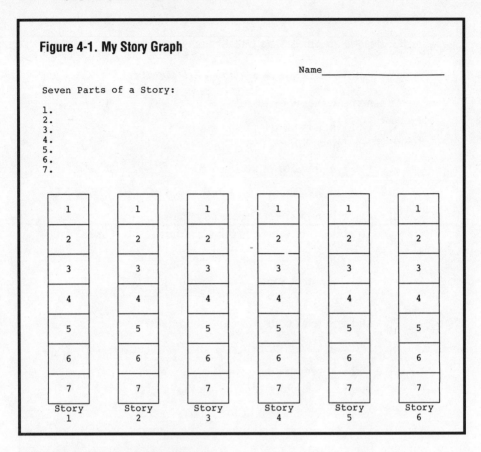

Figure 4-1. My Story Graph

Name_____

Seven Parts of a Story:

1.
2.
3.
4.
5.
6.
7.

1	1	1	1	1	1
2	2	2	2	2	2
3	3	3	3	3	3
4	4	4	4	4	4
5	5	5	5	5	5
6	6	6	6	6	6
7	7	7	7	7	7
Story 1	Story 2	Story 3	Story 4	Story 5	Story 6

Teaching Students to Self-Monitor

Getting students started at self-monitoring, which they then do independently, is relatively easy and usually can be done in about 15-20 minutes. The steps that we use to teach self-monitoring are meant to be used in a flexible way and can be modified to meet teacher and student needs. Finally, while we prefer the teacher and student to collaboratively determine, define, and establish procedures for the behaviors or events to be self- monitored, in some cases it may be necessary for the teacher to tentatively determine and define these before meeting with the student.

Step 1. The first step is to determine and define explicitly what the student will self-monitor. This should be a behavior or event which can be simply defined and easily understood by the student. For example, "to write a good story" might be the student's goal, but this would not be easy for the student to self-monitor. More meaning-fully, the student might self-monitor how many of the seven parts of

Figure 4-2

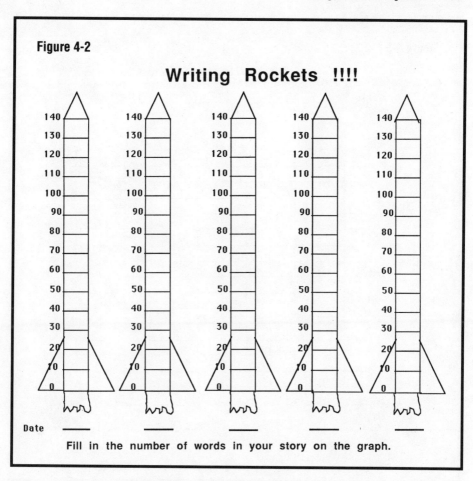

Writing Rockets !!!!

Date

Fill in the number of words in your story on the graph.

a story are included in each of her or his compositions, using a graph such as that in Figure l. Remember that the student must be able to evaluate and record the behavior or event chosen for self-monitoring; monitoring the number of story parts present will not work if the student is not comfortable with the meaning and identification of each part.

Step 2. During the second step, information is gathered on the student's current performance on the behavior or event to be self-assessed. This is done before any self-assessment or self-recording is initiated. This need not be a tedious, time-consuming procedure; often it is sufficient to look at recently written compositions or to have the student write two or three compositions before self-monitoring is introduced. The goal is simply to have enough writing samples to give an accurate picture of current performance. We typically ask the teacher and student to assess and graph targeted aspects of these

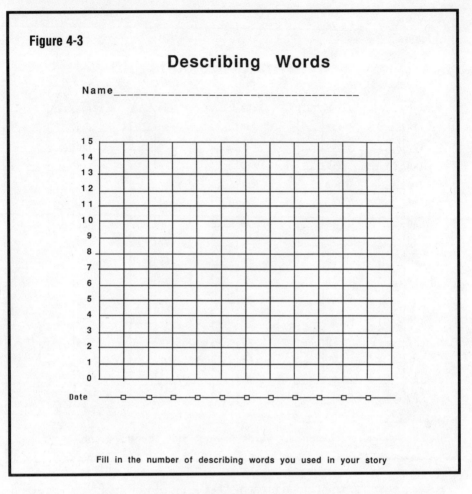

Figure 4-3

Describing Words

Name_____

Fill in the number of describing words you used in your story

compositions in a supportive manner while discussing the current performance level and the benefits of self-monitoring during Step 3. In addition, this baseline data helps to demonstrate progress once the student begins independent self-monitoring. In some cases, however, teachers prefer not to share baseline data with their students because they feel this may be a negative experience for their students. The baseline data is still useful in these situations, however, because it helps teachers assess the effectiveness of self-monitoring.

Step 3. In this step, the teacher briefly explains the rationale for self-monitoring and enlists the student's willing cooperation and commitment to self-monitor (self-monitoring is rarely effective if students are forced to do so against their will). The teacher briefly describes the purpose of self-monitoring and the benefits the student will derive. We typically begin by saying something like, "I would like to teach you something that will help you to help yourself write good stories." The student is then reminded that good stories have seven parts, and the compositions gathered in Step 2 are examined in a positive, collaborative manner and the number of parts in each graphed. The benefits of independently self-monitoring the number of story parts included in future compositions are then discussed.

Students can often name many of the benefits of self-monitoring (for example, "I won't forget to have all of the parts," "I'll like my stories better," "You'll enjoy my stories more," "Writing stories will be more fun," and so on). When evaluating the self-monitoring procedures later with their teachers, it is not unusual for students to mention additional benefits not foreseen when self-monitoring began. For instance, several students whom we taught to self-monitor the parts of a story later reported that this helped them in reading because they watched for the parts as they read. Teachers should not, however, make sweeping promises about the benefits students will derive. For some students, self-monitoring alone may not be effective. These students may need to learn other strategies for writing, such as goal setting or the planning and revising strategies presented in Chapter 3.

Step 4. When the purpose of self-monitoring is clear and the student has indicated willingness to self-monitor, the teacher instructs the student in the procedures involved. It is important that the student has a clear understanding of what is expected, as the student will be self-monitoring independently. Thus, in this step, the teacher and student discuss: (a) what will be self-assessed (for example, the number of story parts, or the planning process); (b) what criteria are desirable (to have all seven parts, or to use a pre-writing planning strategy, for example); (c) how to count (or time) and record the targeted aspect of writing, and (d) when self-monitoring is to occur (for example, it is okay to list and mark off the story parts as you write, then count up the number of parts when you have finished your story and put the number on your graph; be sure to fill in your graph after each story is completed).

After outlining these steps for the student, the teacher (or another student proficient at self-monitoring) models them for the student, verbalizing what is being done at each step. Then the teacher asks the student to talk the teacher through each step, and finally the student models the procedures and verbalizes the steps independently. These last steps are important to be sure that the student clearly understands the self-monitoring procedures as well as the behavior or event to be self-monitored and can carry out the self-monitoring procedures independently. Before the student begins to self-monitor independently, the teacher and student should decide on a date and time to evaluate how self-monitoring is working and how the student likes it.

Once the student begins to self-monitor independently, the teacher should check to see if the student is carrying out the steps properly. If confusion or problems exist, it may be necessary to have a short booster session with the teacher or another student to review or reteach parts of the process. For some students it may initially be helpful to provide a list of steps as a reminder. It is important that the student carry out the self-monitoring procedures correctly and on a regular basis. Once the student has agreed to self-monitor, self-monitoring should occur until the teacher and student agree that it is no longer necessary.

Surprisingly, research consistently indicates that for most students the self-recorded data need not be highly accurate in order for positive effects to occur! When self-monitoring appears to be an appropriate activity, but does not improve performance, then it may be necessary to teach the student to self-record more accurately, or to provide feedback and reinforcement (preferably social reinforcement, such as positive comments) for accurate self-monitoring.

Practical Guidelines

It is important to remember that self-monitoring is not a learning strategy. It is not used to teach or develop writing skills. Thus, in order for self-monitoring to have meaningful effects, students must first be able to perform the writing process or create the writing product to be self-monitored. However, as we mentioned earlier, self-monitoring can be effectively combined with other instructional approaches, including strategy instruction. Self-monitoring can also be enhanced with self-instructions, such as the problem definition and self-evaluation statements discussed earlier in this chapter. For example, a student might ask herself, and then answer, such questions as "Review my goal — how am I doing? Do I need to do anything differently?"

For most students, self-monitoring alone can be effective with some writing processes and products. It is important to note that self-monitoring should not be combined with rewards (such as tokens, stickers, or recess time) that are contingent on performance and based on students' self-records. Providing rewards based on students' self-records provides them with an incentive to "cheat," or inflate their scores, and can lead to inaccurate self-recording. In addition, such an approach places the emphasis on obtaining the reward, rather than on self-regulation. When reinforcers based on students' self-records are not used, researchers have found that students' self-records are typically highly accurate.

Finally, although the student is running the intervention, it is important that the teacher show interest in and regularly review the students' self-recorded data and provide positive social reinforcement for the students' efforts and achievements. When the teacher is appreciative and self-monitoring is enjoyable, students are willing to self-record over long periods of time. We have worked with students who have engaged in self-monitoring for two to three months and have chosen to continue self-monitoring when the teacher felt they could stop if they wanted to do so. Thus, determining when to terminate self-monitoring or to switch to self-monitoring of a new process or behavior should be done collaboratively with the student.

SELF-REINFORCEMENT

The final self-regulation procedure to be examined is self-reinforcement. Self-reinforcement occurs when students choose and administer reinforcers to themselves whenever a criterion for performance has been met or surpassed. Researchers have found that self-reinforcement can be used alone, and that when used alone it is typically as effective as teacher-controlled reinforcement. In some instances, self-reinforcement has had even greater effects than teacher-delivered reinforcement.

For self-reinforcement to truly occur, the student must have full control over available reinforcers and freely impose contingencies for the self-administration of these reinforcers. This must be done in the relative absence of any external controlling influences (in other words, without the teacher's supervision). In classroom settings, such a pure form of self-reinforcement may not be possible, at least initially. As with the development of all self-regulation processes, the transition from teacher (or parent) evaluation and reinforcement to self-evaluation and reinforcement should be a gradual one.

This parallels the natural development of other self-regulation processes. At first, the young child's interactions with parents, teachers, and others provide the basis for setting standards for reinforcement of behavior or performance. Meeting or exceeding these standards typically produces a positive response from parents or others (whereas failing to meet the standards may produce either little response or a negative response). Gradually, the child comes to respond to her or his own behavior in self-rewarding (or self-punishing) ways. While we do not advocate teaching students to self-punish (while mild self-punishment can be a helpful part of self-regulation, some of our students are too good at this as it is), helping students learn to self-reinforce, or improving upon the self-reinforcement processes they already have in place, is an important part of the development of self-regulated learners. In addition, students respond very positively to self-reinforcement procedures, and usually prefer self-determined consequences to externally determined consequences.

We would like to note that in our work on developing writing skills among students, we typically do not teach students to use self-reinforcement alone. Rather, we teach students to self-reinforce in conjunction with the other types of self-management procedures discussed in this chapter. Further, we have found that many students do not need self-administration of tangible (food, stickers, and so on) or activity (time for art work, extra recess, and so on) rewards to improve their writing. Although we have no objection to the use of tangible and activity reinforcers when needed (or the use of a token economy in earning such rewards), the majority of students with whom we have worked have responded very well to learning to use self-reinforcing statements (such as those discussed in the previous section of this chapter on self-instructions and seen in Table 1) in combination with either goal-setting or self-monitoring, or both.

The use of positive self-statements to reward performance follows naturally from both goal setting and self-monitoring. In fact, it is hard to imagine students reaching their goals or self-monitoring their writing as it improves and not engaging in positive self-statements! The use of positive self-statements as a form of self-reinforcement usually comes easily to students, and can be taught through discussion and modeling (see Table 4 for examples of self-reinforcing statements). Thus, we next discuss teaching students to self-reinforce, followed by a discussion of practical guidelines and issues in the use of self-reinforcement in the classroom.

Teaching Students to Self-Reinforce

Students can learn both to self-reinforce during the writing process and to provide self-reinforcement for the writing product. Aspects of the writing process and product that might be targeted for self-regulation were listed in the previous section of this chapter concern-

Table 4-4. REWARD YOURSELF!!!! SAY SOMETHING NICE!!!

AWESOME!
THAT WAS MY BEST JOB!
WONDERFUL!
OUTSTANDING!
SPLENDID!
FANTASTIC JOB!
EXCELLENT! KEEP UP THE GOOD WORK!
WOW!
TERRIFIC!
GREAT!
NICE JOB!
WELL DONE!
GOOD JOB!
TERRIFIC!
SUPER!
I'M A GENIUS!

ing self-monitoring; these same aspects are appropriate for self-reinforcement.

Adult writers frequently use self-reinforcement to maintain and improve their writing performance. For instance, another way Ernest Hemingway reportedly rewarded himself for particularly productive writing days (in lieu of the night on the town noted earlier), was by going fishing on the Gulf Stream the following day. Reaching his standards for a highly productive day allowed him to enjoy a day of fishing without feeling guilty.

Self-reinforcement basically involves four components: (1) determining the standards for earning a reward, (2) selecting the reinforcer to be earned, (3) evaluating performance, and (4) self-administering the reinforcer. Students can gradually assume partial or total responsibility for all of these components, depending upon their age and maturity.

As we noted at the beginning of this chapter, self-regulation processes are interrelated and typically occur in combination. Thus, self-reinforcement involves a simple form of goal setting (setting standards worthy of reward) as well as self-evaluation; while goal setting and self-monitoring can occur without self-reinforcement, self-reinforcement necessarily involves components of both. Helping students learn to establish self-determined criteria was discussed in the previous section of this chapter on goal setting; self-evaluation was discussed in the section on self-monitoring.

We suggest that students learn to self-reinforce by initially collaborating with the teacher on the four components we've listed; beginning with one component at a time. It is not uncommon for students to have a say in the reinforcer they wish to earn. To begin the transfer to self-reinforcement, the teacher and student together can determine what level of performance will earn what amount of reinforcement. For example, if increasing the number of arguments presented in a student's opinion essays is an important goal, then the teacher and student can collaborate on the standards for reinforcement. If the student has expressed a desire to earn extra time for art activities, then the teacher and student might look at the student's current writing and determine that a certain number of arguments presented, let's say two, earns five minutes of art time. While the teacher might initially be responsible for determining the number of arguments presented and arranging the extra time for art activities, the teacher and student can collaborate on the gradual sharing of responsibility for these procedures as well. When appropriate, full control over one or more of the four components involved in self-reinforcement can gradually be transferred to the student, with the teacher perhaps acting primarily as an observer.

Guidelines and Issues

One of the first issues to be faced in teaching students to self-reinforce is student determination of standards of performance deserving of reward. Many students initially need assistance here. Some students will tend to set more lenient performance standards for themselves than those set by their teachers. Stringent standards, however, typically produce better academic performance than do lenient standards.

We use the term stringent on an individual basis here; what is a stringent standard, say for number of arguments presented for one student, may be a lenient standard for another student. Students who set lenient standards for themselves may need to be prompted to set stringent standards, or may need to collaborate with the teacher in determining standards. These students might be helped to set progressively more stringent standards for themselves, particularly if they lack conviction that they can meet such standards or if they experience a great deal of anxiety about writing.

On the other hand, some students will tend to set standards for performance that will be difficult for them to achieve, thus lessening their chances of self-administering the reinforcer. These students will need assistance in setting reasonable and attainable standards. Remember that self-reinforcement is not a teaching procedure; in other words, students should not be using self-reinforcement for writing processes or products they do not know how to achieve.

A related issue is self-evaluation. Here again, some students will tend to be harder on themselves than their teachers would be when judging their performance on writing processes or their writing products. Other students will no doubt be easier on themselves than would their teachers. Thus, many students will need to collaborate with the teacher to obtain accurate self-evaluations. Self-evaluation can be particularly difficult for students when less objective aspects of writing are being assessed, such as how persuasive an essay is or how much elaboration is provided for story parts. It may be wise, therefore, to begin self-reinforcement with more objective aspects of writing, such as the number of arguments included in a persuasive composition or opinion essay, or the amount of time spent writing.

The process of self-reinforcement can be facilitated if the procedures to be followed are detailed and specific. The procedures to be followed might be agreed upon by the teacher and student and recorded so the student has a written set of steps to follow if needed. In addition, it is important to note that student self-reinforcement does not mean that teacher reinforcement, particularly forms of social reinforcement such as praise, a hug, shaking hands, positive feedback, or a smile or wink, should end. Quite the contrary. Social reinforcement from the teacher, including reinforcement for engaging in self-reinforcement, continues to be important, as does social reinforcement from peers and parents. Over time, students who choose tangible or activity reinforcers for self-administration should be encouraged to make use of self-praise and good feelings about their writing as well. Gradually, such forms of self-reinforcement may largely replace tangible and activity reinforcers, although it should be remembered that even adult writers frequently make use of such reinforcers, as did Ernest Hemingway.

Finally, we would like to note that some research indicates that motivational characteristics may be an important factor in determining the success of self-reinforcement. Students who are strongly motivated by feelings of self-satisfaction and who attribute their successes and failures to their level of effort (or lack thereof) may take easily to self-reinforcement procedures and find that these procedures make a difference in their writing. On the other hand, students who emphasize the importance of external contingencies and agencies may have more trouble with effective use of self-reinforcement. This does not mean that self-reinforcement should not be used with these students; in fact, developing self-reinforcement capabilities may help these students come to be more motivated by feelings of self-satisfaction and to recognize the importance of their own efforts. These students, however, may need a more gradual transition from teacher reinforcement to self-reinforcement and may need more assistance in mastering the components of self-reinforcement. Full-blown self-regulated strategy development, as described in Chapters Two and Five, can include self-reinforcement and may help many students along the way to becoming self-regulated writers.

CHAPTER FIVE

Self-Regulated Strategy Development: Planning for Success

In this chapter we expand on the instructional model presented in Chapter 2. Specifically, we discuss aspects of planning and implementing self-regulated strategy development. By doing so, we take another look at what happens during strategy instruction and the benefits of this approach. Seven basic, but interrelated and recursive, planning stages that allow teachers to maximize the individualization and power of strategy instruction are recommended. The relationships among these seven stages can be seen in Figure 1.

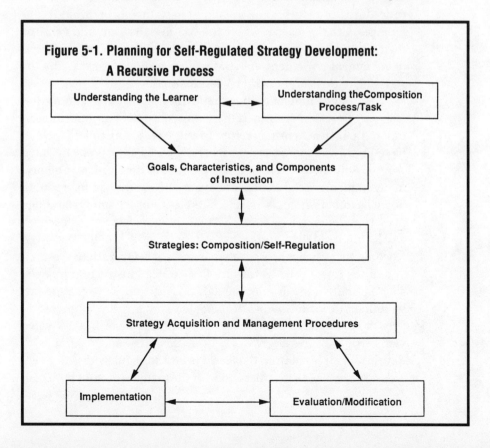

Figure 5-1. Planning for Self-Regulated Strategy Development: A Recursive Process

While these seven planning stages are important to successful strategy instruction for all students, aspects of the first four stages are particularly critical for teachers working with students experiencing writing or other learning problems in terms of skills, processes, or attitudes. Thus, these four stages are discussed in detail in this chapter. The fifth stage, determining strategy acquisition and management procedures, was discussed in Chapter 2. Stages six and seven are discussed in Chapter 6.

UNDERSTANDING THE LEARNER AND THE COMPOSITION PROCESS/TASK

As with all forms of effective teaching, self-regulated strategy development begins with a thorough understanding of both the learner and the task, an understanding that is further enhanced as teacher and students work together. Careful, ongoing understanding of the learner and the task allows flexible and individualized selection and tailoring of instructional goals, components, characteristics, and procedures. Students act as collaborators at this stage through conferences with the teacher where they discuss the topic and genre of their writing, as well as their goals both for their work and their development as writers. As strategy instruction proceeds, understanding of the learner and task is enhanced.

Although understanding the learner and understanding the task are discussed separately here, in reality the two inform each other. Again, teachers may return to any stage at any time. Teachers have an advantage over researchers here, as they typically have worked with their students for some period of time and have gained many valuable insights and understandings. Strategy instruction, however, often demands that teachers broaden their understandings of their students, as it requires that multiple perspectives on teaching and learning be taken, and that new understandings of the learning/ teaching process be incorporated as they develop both in research and in the classroom. As this implies, strategy instruction models, such as our own, are developmental and will continue to change and be refined over time. Our self-regulated strategy development approach has undergone a great deal of development in the twelve years that we have been working in this area, and continues to develop as we learn from the teachers and students with whom we work. We turn now to a discussion of the many aspects of both task and learner that we have found valuable to consider in determining the goals, characteristics, components, and procedures involved in strategy instruction; this discussion is not all-inclusive, but provides a good beginning.

THE LEARNER

Age and Development

Strategy instruction must be in line with the learner's chronological age, cognitive capacities, and development. Researchers have found that these factors influence the form, content, and rate of instruction. It is important to note that the composition strategies we have validated and present in this book, and our self-regulated strategy development approach in general, are typically meant for students in the fourth grade and above. Among the reasons for this are students' development of memory and other information processing capabilities and their development of the abilities underlying writing processes and an understanding of writing. As students enter the upper elementary grades and make the transition from elementary to middle grades and later to high school, they face increasing demands for writing and knowledge of writing genres. They are expected both to learn and to communicate through writing, and face such assignments as book reports, biographies, integrative reviews, opinion essays, persuasive essays, science project reports, and so on. Mastery of powerful writing strategies can be a significant aid in their advancement as learners.

Some students will be ready for and able to profit from composition strategy instruction before the fourth grade. Teachers we have worked with have indicated their third and even second graders have typically found composition strategies helpful. They have also reported that these students have more difficulty memorizing the strategy components and coming to use them flexibly and in a sophisticated manner; thus, they have sometimes modified the strategies to make them more developmentally appropriate and have provided memory aids through bulletin boards, charts, and other concrete reminders of the strategy mnemonic or procedures. Younger students and those who experience severe difficulties with composition may also need more extensive preskill development, more explicit instructional components and procedures, or more scaffolding (teacher support).

Beliefs, Attitudes, Attributions, and Expectancies

It is also important to consider students' attitudes, beliefs, attributions, and expectancies. This is particularly critical for those students who have experienced a history of failure in academics generally or in writing specifically. Students who have experienced significant learning problems frequently develop a complex set of negative, maladaptive beliefs and expectancies that interact with ongoing experiences, resulting in low motivation, attitudinal problems, and lessened effort. Repeated failure can result in a student's believing that he or she is lacking in ability and is not capable of overcoming the difficulties faced. In other words, it can result in feelings of helplessness, often referred to as "learned helplessness",and can result in lowered expectancies for future success. Students' beliefs about their capabilities can further affect their efforts and achievement. If a student believes that continued effort in the face of difficulty is likely to lead to success, he or she is likely to persevere. If, on the other hand, the student believes that further effort will have little effect, he or she is most likely to quit, even when the task is do-able.

Self-efficacy. Researchers have investigated the effects of students' beliefs and expectancies from a number of interrelated perspectives, including attributions, locus of control, and self-efficacy. The term *self-efficacy* is used to refer to students' pre-task judgments, their expectancies of whether they can perform a given task or activity. Some researchers believe that change in self-efficacy is the common underlying cognitive process that accounts for changes in behavior. Self-efficacy is believed to have a strong influence on performance as it affects choice of activities, the amount of effort expended, and persistence in the face of difficulty. In other words, individuals who believe they are capable of successful performance are likely to choose challenging activities, work hard, and persist when difficulties are encountered. We are only just beginning to understand the role of self-efficacy in children's learning. Interestingly, very young children and students with learning problems frequently exhibit unrealistically high pre-task expectancies; they expect to be able to successfully complete activities that they are not yet capable of. Unrealistically high expectancies among students with learning problems may be due to misperceptions of task demands or difficulty in comprehending the task, inaccurate self-knowledge, selective attention to what they have mastered, ignoring what they have not, inability to match demands to ability level, or employing a self-protective coping strategy. When unrealistically high pre-task expectancies are followed by failure, negative, maladaptive attitudes and beliefs may be strengthened.

Causal attributions. Causal attributions are explanations given for one's own successes and failures. When students believe that their difficulties are due to stable factors beyond their control, particularly inability, they typically exhibit less effort, use less sophisticated strategies than they are capable of, and perform below their capabilities.

Failure typically results in feelings of distress. Students who attribute their failure(s) to insufficient ability experience higher levels of distress and negative affect than those who attribute failure to factors within their control. Students who attribute their difficulties to factors within their control, particularly insufficient effort, tend to persist and maintain strategic performance when they face difficulties. We sometimes find that difficulty prompts these students to use or create strategies more sophisticated than those they had used previously.

Locus of control. Locus of control is also related to causal beliefs. Researchers have found that a generally internal locus of control tends to be more adaptive than a generalized external locus of control. An internal locus of control is said to exist when an individual typically attributes successes and failures to controllable factors that reside within oneself (such as effort, the development of skills and capabilities, and so on), rather than to external factors. A student with an external locus of control might typically attribute failure to bad luck, other people (the teacher doesn't like me), or task difficulty (this is too hard for me), even when the task is within her or his grasp. Although at this point in time researchers have focused primarily on ability, effort, task difficulty and luck as the four causes perceived as most responsible for success and failure, a host of other attributions for success and failure can exist as well, such as mood, fatigue, attention, the level to which an activity is valued, previous experiences, or the presence of a handicapping condition such as learning disabilities.

It is important at this point to note two things. First, the words "typically," "tend," and "generally" are used quite a bit in the preceding paragraphs on attributions and locus of control. Although causal beliefs that attribute success and failure to internal, controllable factors are desirable, no student (or adult either, for that matter) should be expected to express only these beliefs. There are times when it is accurate to believe that external or uncontrollable factors are related to success and failure, and it could be unhealthy to have too strong an internal locus of control. In real life there are frequently multiple factors that contribute to one's successes and failures. For example, in explaining a particular achievement, one might say, "I worked hard and I was lucky." Second, the tendency toward an internal locus of control is developmental. Very young children typically exhibit a more external locus of control, which becomes more internal as they grow and develop.

Self-diagnosed poor writers. Writing instruction does not take place in a vacuum. Rather, instruction takes place in the context of school; a context that is both physical and social. Classrooms differ physically and teachers differ in expectations, goals, and values, in their views about acceptable and unacceptable behavior, and in their teaching styles. Thus, an important aspect of understanding the attitudes and beliefs of the learner relates to understanding previous and current contexts for learning, and the students' previous experiences with writing and writing instruction.

We prefer writing strategy instruction to take place within the context of a process-oriented approach. Students whose writing instruction has occurred in the context of a product-oriented approach, and particularly those students who have experienced difficulty or failure with the mechanics of writing, may initially need greater support. They may have come to believe that they are poor writers; their difficulties with mechanics may have convinced them that they lack worthwhile ideas and experiences to communicate to others.

Other predilections and characteristics. It is helpful to consider other aspects of the learner such as the student's tolerance for frustration, ambiguity, errors, and difficulty. What temperaments are evident among the students? Are they impulsive responders? How do they handle anger and other emotions? Do they experience high writing anxiety or fear of writing? Have they had experience with and are they willing to collaborate in problem solving? Do they make use of resources such as peers, teachers, and materials? Do they approach tasks and activities in an organized, structured way and share in responsibility for their own learning? What self-regulation abilities do the students have, and what self-management strategies are developing? What types of self-speech (positive and negative) do the students use—out loud or covert? The answers to these questions can inform strategy instruction, influencing the goals of instruction and affecting the choice of components and procedures as well as the characteristics of instruction.

Students' metacognitive skills should also be considered, including their self-awareness and ability to assess a situation or task, identify available relevant strategies, choose among alternatives, develop a plan, monitor performance, and modify cognitive activities as necessary. Strategy instruction must often be aimed at the development of metacognition as well as mastery of powerful strategies. Understanding students' initial knowledge states and abilities is critical; otherwise, students may be taught a strategy less efficient or no better than the one(s) they are already using, or one that is beyond their cognitive-development abilities.

Response of strategy instruction. What does all of this mean to us in terms of strategy instruction? First, students who have experienced frequent failure may come to the classroom or to the writing task with maladaptive beliefs, attitudes, attributions, and expectancies. This belief system may be strong enough to inhibit a student from engaging in an activity they can do successfully. The student will experience great difficulty developing as a writer unless this belief system is addressed directly. Second, the self-regulated strategy development approach developed and tailored for these students should include components that help to break the vicious cycle of negative beliefs, self-perceptions, attitudes, expectancies, and experiences these students are caught up in.

What are these components? First, choose a powerful strategy appropriate to the learner's developmental level, needs, and interests — a strategy that can actually mediate successful performance. Second, choose writing tasks and goals that are also appropriate for the learner (here it is easy to see how critical the match of learner and task can be). Third, help the student gradually to develop more positive, adaptive attributions and expectancies. This can be accomplished in several ways. For example, in the conferences and discussions that occur before strategy instruction begins, the teacher and students can discuss how the students' current strategies (or lack of strategies) impede successful performance; how the proposed strategy is helpful; what students can expect in terms of their writing when they master this strategy; and the fact that effort and commitment will be necessary to learn the strategy. Discussions that help students identify any negative, maladaptive self-statements they use, followed by the development of effective, adaptive self-instructions during strategy instruction can also help. Commitment on the student's part to collaborate in the mastery of the strategy is also important—forcing students into strategy instruction is rarely effective in our experience.

Goal setting, self-assessment, and self-recording also help; these self-regulation activities allow students to experience self-control and to see visibly the results of their efforts and mastery of the strategy. Discussions with students throughout strategy instruction can help to establish the important role their efforts in mastering, implementing, evaluating (and modifying, if appropriate) the strategy have played in their development as writers. Finally, we have found that experiencing control of an effective strategy, success in meeting one's goals, and pleasure in the process and outcome of the writing experience are quite effective in helping to create new adaptive attitudes, beliefs, attributions, and experiences.

Gaining understanding. Although there may seem to be many learner characteristics that need to be considered, the task is not as difficult as it may appear at first. Teachers can come to understand best the dynamic processes involved in their students' thinking and learning by working and talking with them. Assessment of students' cognitive and affective states needs to occur before, throughout, and after strategy instruction; some changes may take a considerable amount of time and experiences to manifest. Interviews, conferences, and discussions are helpful in gaining insight. Having students think aloud while completing the writing task may also be of help. Some students, however, may have trouble communicating cognitions verbally; as we have seen, self-awareness is a skill that must be acquired.

Observing and keeping notes on responses to questions, approaches, and probes can also be helpful, as can manipulating characteristics of the task (modality, rate of presentation, support, and so on) or creating modified versions of the task that help to illuminate a student's task approach. Evaluating what works and what doesn't work as strategy instruction proceeds can also provide valuable insights.

Teachers who are aware of important cognitive and affective characteristics gain an increased understanding of their students as they work with them, and are able to use this understanding in the design and modification of cognitive strategy instruction. Students with learning problems often have the greatest needs in terms of support for change in the affective and cognitive characteristics underlying learning. Goals of instruction, however, must be kept within reasonable expectations. This sort of change is a developmental process that takes time. Self-regulated strategy development can play an important role in this change and development.

Oral and Written Language

If modeling and self-instructions are to be part of the instructional package, then the students' language style and development need to be carefully considered. The model's performance should be matched to the students' expressive and receptive language as well as idiosyncratic preferences. Thus, for some students it may be appropriate to model a statement such as, "One of the first things I have to do is think about the main characters for my story," while for others it may be appropriate to model a statement such as, "Ok, step 1, who is my story about?" Once students have observed the model's performance, they will need to develop their own self-instructions in their own words (see Chapter 4).

Specific language skills important in mastering the strategy to be taught need to be considered, such as understanding of vocabulary words and concepts. Sometimes we have found that previous experiences have resulted in negative attitudes among students regarding certain terms and aspects of writing. For instance, remember the student in Chapter 3 who believed that he could not learn to enhance the use of adjectives, verbs, and adverbs in his writing because he had failed those topics in English. We did not push the issue. Later, when a strategy aimed at enhancing planning and communication in writing through use of describing words, action words, and action helpers was introduced, this same student voiced no objections and did quite well (and was quite amazed to learn later that describing words were also called adjectives, etc.)

It is also important to have a good understanding of students' writing skills and capabilities. What do the students know about writing processes, including brainstorming, planning, translating, revising, and editing? About how written language is different from oral language? What strengths and problems do students exhibit in comprehending writing demands and tasks? Do some of the students possess knowledge or strategies that are not spontaneously produced and applied when they could be useful? What strategies do they currently produce, and do these strategies effectively mediate performance? What strategies are just beyond their capabilities alone, but could be used effectively with support? The answers to these questions will help to shape the goals and content of current and future instruction.

Students who have already mastered effective composition strategies or developed their own can be asked to share these with others. Teachers also need to be aware of the broad range of skills, abilities, real world knowledge, specialized knowledge, topics of interest, solutions to writing problems, and writing styles represented within their writing community so they and their students can draw on these resources. Finally, teachers need to know the state of each student's mechanical skills, so these skills can be developed within the context of meaning and communication. Teachers can help students come to understand that improved mechanical skills, such as spelling, punctuation, and paragraph development, can play an important role in their communication with readers.

THE TASK

A thorough understanding of the task both informs and is informed by the understanding of the learner. The affective demands of the task and the cognitions involved in effective performance need to be understood. Component cognitive strategies and the cognitive abilities required need to be identified. The resulting understanding of the task coupled with the understanding of the learner greatly facilitates the next stage in our model of self-regulated strategy development—determining the goals, characteristics, and components of the strategy instruction.

Cognitive Demands

Developing understanding of the writing task requires consideration of the genre as well as the planning, translating, producing, revising, and editing processes involved in the writing task. As the cognitive processes required by the writing task become more numerous and complex, task difficulty increases and greater cognitive capacity is needed. For example, as composition strategies become more sophisticated and complex, greater demands are placed on the student's memory and information processing abilities. Cognitions involved in comprehension of the writing task (identifying the problem and the goal), the production of appropriate strategies, and the application, monitoring, evaluation, and revision of these strategies (in other words, metacognitive skills) should be considered. In addition to these cognitive demands, preskills relevant to both the writing task and the successful regulation of the composition strategy need to be identified.

Determining preskills and cognitions involved in effective performance can be done in several ways. One is to observe and question experts before, during, and after composition processes. The experts can include students (of differing ages and abilities) and adults, as well as the teacher. These individuals can be asked to report the skills, strategies, and other cognitions (self-speech, imagery, expectancies, and so on) that they experience and employ. Individuals who have difficulty with composition processes or self-regulation might also be interviewed and observed in order to speculate on what leads to poor performance. Further information regarding preskills and cognitions evident among experts and students experiencing difficulty might be gained by manipulating aspects of the task (problem or goal, use of cues and prompts, level of teacher support, and so on) or by creating modified versions of the task. Finally, literature concerning effective, validated cognitive strategies for composition and self-regulation processes (such as those presented in this book and the other books in this series) can be consulted.

Affective Demands

Affective demands of the composition task may include coping with errors, complexity, difficulty, ambiguity, and so on. The task may be likely to create frustration, anger, or other emotions. It is helpful to consider potentially positive or negative interactions between the affective demands of the task and students' characteristics. For example, a particular student may evidence a low tolerance for frustration, while the composition task may produce a potentially high level of frustration due to complexity and demands on memory and information processing. A mnemonic, charts or other prompts, or extensive scaffolding may initially be needed to alleviate or moderate these demands. On the other hand, mastery of a powerful composition strategy can produce feelings of competence and pride in the writing process and the products it enables the student to generate. Ways to enhance affective responses such as these should be determined.

Because writing in the classroom takes place in a social context, it is also important to consider affective demands of the task in relation to the student body as a whole. One of the goals of a process approach to writing is to create a community of learners. Teachers and students may be able to identify ways in which individuals in the classroom can help to moderate affective demands by acting as sources of support, providing feedback or ideas, or allowing venting of emotions. One of the teachers with whom we have worked noted that one thing several of her students needed most was an appropriate, positive way to deal with their feelings regarding constructive criticism or feedback from peers or the teacher; the need to revise or edit a manuscript also seemed to evoke negative emotions for some students.

Linkages

What are the linkages between the composition task and strategies and the larger context and content of learning? Understanding how this composition task and related self-regulation abilities link to other writing tasks and other areas of the curriculum will facilitate teacher and student planning for generalization to other settings and tasks and maintenance of strategic performance over time. This understanding also promotes development of a maximally powerful strategy and strategy instruction procedures.

Aspects of the writing task under consideration may be evident in other writing tasks and in reading others' writing (in the form of books, stories, journals, science reports, and so on). Aspects of the task may be relevant to demands faced in many areas of the curriculum, such as reading literature and writing reviews or reports in English classes, reading and writing biographies or other forms of non-fiction in social studies classes, or experiment and project reports in science classes. Consideration of topic, audience, and purpose is relevant to nearly all forms of written language.

The metacognitive skills and capabilities discussed in Chapter 4 and frequently embedded in composition strategy instruction are relevant across the curriculum as well as in non-content areas such as academic self-management (being organized, responsible and persistent) and social interactions. Understanding the linkages between the task under consideration and the larger context of learning will enable the teacher to identify a variety of contexts, materials, situations, and settings relevant to the goals of strategy instruction, particularly goals regarding maintenance and generalizatlon. These goals are discussed further in the next section.

DETERMINING GOALS AND COMPONENTS OF INSTRUCTION

Although the seven stages in our self-regulated strategy development model are presented sequentially in Figure 1, in actuality they may be returned to at any stage at any time and integrated. Developing an understanding of both the learner and the composition process/task informs the determination of the goals, characteristics, and components of strategy instruction. Determination of goals, characteristics, and components then informs and is further informed by the selection of the composition and self-regulation strategies to be taught. Thus, many of the desired goals, characteristics, and components of the strategy instruction being planned will emerge in conjunction with consideration of task and learner; others will be determined after the learner and task have been considered or as the strategies to be taught are determined.

Goals

Establishing goals allows the teacher to tailor learning activities to the desired outcomes. Desired outcomes need to be specified in advance. Affective, cognitive, and metacognitive student characteristics, as well as composition preskills, skills, and processes, can be targeted for change or development during instruction. Instructional targets should depend upon the understanding of both task and learner. The skills and processes targeted for development must be important enough to effect a reasonable change in the student's writing performance, yet within the student's capabilities. The goal is to present a "do-able" challenge—one the student can accomplish given scaffolded instruction of a strategy that, once mastered, mediates successful performance. While independent, self-regulated, strategic performance is an important overall goal, motivation must be considered as well. Strategy instruction should provide students with the skill as well as the will to act strategically.

Instructional goals, however, must be kept within reasonable expectations. The learner and task analyses may lead to the establishment of numerous goals as well as overarching needs. In this case, the teacher will need to determine a reasonable starting point and build from there. We have found that it is generally better to start with modest goals and gradually add affective, cognitive, and composition targets as strategy instruction progresses and as teachers and students become more comfortable with the procedures.

Critical Goals: Maintenance and Generalization

Goals for maintenance and generalization, as well as plans to meet these goals, should be established prior to instruction. Durability is necessary but not sufficient for generalization. We often desire to see the composition and self-regulation strategies students have mastered generalized across tasks, settings, instructors, or other variables. Unfortunately, researchers know relatively little about the breadth, depth, and course of the development of maintenance and generalization capabilities of children. We sometimes have little but intuition to guide us in setting reasonable goals and evaluating outcomes in these areas.

Durability appears easier to obtain than generalization, although reports of generalization are increasing in research literature. The ability to generalize may be related to age, readiness, and metacognitive maturity. Some researchers have found that metacognition relevant to strategy use develops with age and experience. Younger children may be more likely to maintain and generalize skills when the instructional and generalization tasks are concrete and familiar. It also appears that less explicit instruction is needed to promote durable strategy use with older as compared to younger children. Students who are experiencing learning difficulties often appear to be less metacognitively and cognitively mature than their normally achieving counterparts.

Yet researchers have found that teachers can do a great deal to help their students come to own strategies they have mastered—that is, so that their students develop an understanding of where, when, and how to use strategic procedures and are motivated to do so. The following suggestions are from our work and that of other researchers for enhancing durable and generalized use of strategies as strategy instruction occurs:

- Provide instruction that is prolonged and in depth, and conducted by several individuals across a variety of tasks, materials, demands, settings, and conditions. Brief, short-term strategy instruction should not be expected to show long-term generalizable effects.

- Actively involve students in the selection and development of instructional goals and procedures, as well as the acquisition and evaluation of new strategies and skills.

- Actively involve students in the identification of opportunities for generalized use of a strategy, or in the modification of a strategy for generalization purposes.

- Facilitate discussion about the purpose and usefulness of the strategy(s) taught, as well as feedback on the learner's performance.

- Remind students to generalize; provide support and reinforcement for doing so as necessary.

- Facilitate generalization by attributing observed changes to the students' own efforts and strategy mastery.

- Facilitate maintenance by incorporating planned booster sessions into ongoing instruction, by having students who have mastered a strategy instruct others, and so on.

- Emphasize the development of metacognitive, self-regulatory skills.

- Gradually fade teacher or peer support, cues, and prompts to facilitate transfer of strategy control to students.

- Focus on developing skills and strategies that can be maintained by natural contingencies after transfer to a new environment or situation.

- Criterion cheat: Select instructional tasks, goals, and situations similar (but not necessarily identical) to desired generalization tasks and situations.

- If distractors, affective demands, or other significant variables exist in the generalization setting but not in the initial instructional setting, gradually include components and discussions in the instructional setting that will help the student handle these variables in the generalization setting.

- If students spend part of their day with other instructors, cooperation and collaboration regarding strategy use in these classes with these teachers and the students should be developed.

- Engage students in ample opportunities to self-evaluate their learning and performance; help make progress evident through self-monitoring using graphs, establishing portfolios, and so on.

- Establish a family or community support base.

- Emphasize consistency and precision in the initial stages of strategy instruction; once students have mastered a strategy, personalization or modification of the strategy should be encouraged as long as the strategy is not subverted.

- Once students have experienced success with cognitive strategies, help them learn to analyze a novel problem or demand and design their own strategy or adapt a previously learned strategy.

When durability and generalization are incorporated in the goals of strategy instruction from the beginning, and when the suggestions provided are incorporated into instruction to the extent possible, independent, self-regulated, strategic performance is facilitated. Some researchers, however, have found that it may be necessary to differentiate between students who can't generalize and those who can but don't. For the latter students, researchers have found that additional steps may be undertaken successfully. These include a contract between the instructor and student involving self-regulated strategy use in generalization settings or on differing tasks, the use of reinforcement, and more intensive, explicit discussion and instruction regarding generalization and any factors inhibiting generalization.

Components

As we have noted, strategy instruction is typically multicomponent. However, both the number of components and the way in which they are integrated can vary greatly. As we noted earlier, some students may not need strategy instruction, or may need relatively minor forms of support to function strategically. However, we have found that all students can profit from an increased understanding of specific writing strategies, their role in writing, and how to self-regulate their use in writing.

Older or more capable students may respond readily to simpler forms of strategy instruction, such as direct explanation, modeling, and/or collaborative practice. More complex strategy instruction (see Chapter 2) becomes appropriate as the learner's problems become more severe or the goals of instruction become multifaceted and complex (including affective, cognitive, metacognitive, and composition objectives). Students who experience significant problems with composition skills, processes, and negative attitudes or anxieties about either themselves or writing require a higher level of scaffolding, more explicit instruction, and more time for change. Thus, procedures must be developed to help the learner integrate skills, processes, strategies, and self-regulation. When multiple components and procedures are to be used, it may be helpful to begin on tasks at which the learner is somewhat proficient, gradually introducing new components and procedures. Task difficulty and length of instructional sessions can also be gradually increased.

Strategies: Composition and Self-Regulation

The determination of the self-regulation and/or composition strategies to be taught to an individual or a group of students follows from the thorough understanding of the learner and composition process/task and the determination of the goals, characteristics, and components of instruction. In addition, the determination of strategies may reciprocally influence the characteristics and components of instruction. A family of composition strategies that we have validated was presented in Chapter 3. Similarly, a family of self-regulation strategies that can be used individually or in combination was presented in Chapter 4. The difficult aspect of this stage of our model of self-regulated strategy development is the selection of effective composition strategy(s). Although teachers will be able to locate some validated, effective composition strategies by consulting the literature or other resources, they will frequently have to develop or modify strategies appropriate for their own and their students' needs (see Chapter 3).

Strategy instruction is an emerging approach, and a great many more strategies remain to be studied and developed. Great care must be taken to ensure that the selected, adapted, or devised strategy works; otherwise well-intentioned teachers may unwittingly teach strategies that do not work well. Unfortunately, a great many traditional and newly developed strategies are recommended or packaged and sold without empirical validation of their efficacy. This has become increasingly evident as strategy instruction has become more recognized as a viable instructional approach. Thus, teachers must be cautious consumers.

In addition to being cautious consumers, teachers must also act as strategy evaluators and validators. Even empirically proven strategies may need modification to be maximally effective for certain individuals or local needs. Teachers should continually assess the utility or power of the strategies they are recommending their students use. Given the importance of the evaluation and validation of both strategies and strategy acquisition procedures, we have devoted the next chapter to this topic (Chapter 6). We then conclude this book with a brief discussion of how self-regulated strategy instruction helps students come to learn "the trick of it."

CHAPTER SIX

Evaluating Strategy and Strategy Instruction Effectiveness

One aspect of strategy instruction that is often slighted or overlooked is evaluation. Children and their parents have every right to expect that strategies taught at school really do work. It is all too possible, however, to unwittingly teach students strategies that simply do not work or do not work well, or to go about strategy instruction in ineffective ways. Such troubling situations can be avoided by making evaluation of the processes used to teach the strategy and changes in students' performance a routine part of instruction.

Unfortunately, many school systems do little to help make evaluation part of the instructional process. Rather, most school testing programs concentrate on taking "snapshots" of students' performance. Students are periodically assembled during the school year and given norm-referenced, standardized academic tests. These tests provide little information that teachers can actually use in the classroom. The best way that teachers can collect useful assessment information is by monitoring how the instructional program affects what their students do.

Why are such classroom evaluations not more common? Part of the answer to this question involves how schools are organized. Making formal and informal evaluation procedures an integral part of teaching requires time to design and carry out assessments, as well as time to interpret and reflect on the results. Additional time is also needed to make use of the results, applying them to make needed changes in the instructional program. This is difficult to do in most schools since very little time is provided for these activities.

Since schools do not adequately support and reward teachers for such evaluations, are we off-base in recommending that teachers make this an integral part of teaching? We don't think so for several reasons. First, monitoring and evaluating the effects of instructional efforts is important to teachers' intellectual and professional growth. Teachers who closely assess what they are doing and how things are going are better able to direct and regulate the teaching process.

Teachers without such information are much more likely to be controlled by the materials or curriculum they use, failing to recognize when things are not working out. Likewise, ongoing evaluation of classroom processes provides teachers with a way of learning more about themselves and their students. Reflecting on what happens in the classroom and how they and their students react provides teachers with considerable insight into what they are doing and what adjustments they should make in their instruction.

Ongoing classroom evaluation is also important to student growth. If teachers are unaware that their instructional methods are not working with some or all of their students and simply carry on, students may come to devalue themselves as learners or to devalue the content and skills being taught. For example, students who are taught a strategy that does not improve their performance will not be enthusiastic about learning a second strategy. They may also interpret lack of improvement as an indication of their incompetence, rather than as indicative of a weakness in the strategy or its instruction. In addition, when students act as collaborators and have access to ongoing evaluation data, they are more likely to become active participants in their own educational growth.

PRINCIPLES IN EVALUATION

The following is a list of principles for evaluating the effectiveness of strategies and the procedures used to teach them. While the list is surely not exhaustive, it includes principles we have found to be useful in assessing strategy instruction in the area of writing.

The Amount of Evidence Collected Depends on the Established Effectiveness of the Strategy

The basic tenet of this principle is that a newly developed strategy needs to be more closely assessed than a strategy that repeatedly has been shown to be effective in the past. This same rule applies to the methods used to help students develop mastery of the strategy. Methods that have been previously validated (not just by researchers but also in the teacher's classroom) need less scrutiny than newly devised methods or procedures being used for the first time. The essential point is that the amount of time and effort expended on this aspect of evaluation depends on the established validity of the strategy and teaching methods used and the teacher's history with both.

While we encourage teachers to use empirically validated strategies, the list of writing (and other) strategies that have been empirically validated is short. Thus, teachers often find it necessary to adopt or adapt existing strategies, such as the ones in this book, or develop new ones based on a thorough understanding of the task, their students, and the composing processes underlying effective writing (as discussed in Chapter Five). When they are devising a new strategy, we encourage teachers to try out the procedure with a few students. A reasonably economical way of achieving this goal is for the teacher to describe and model the strategy for several students to see if they can use it successfully and effectively. These students can serve as collaborators, providing feedback and suggestions for evaluating and modifying the strategy. Once the strategy is working well for the teacher and the student collaborators, teaching the strategy to other students (perhaps with the student collaborators acting as peer tutors) is warranted.

Even with well-validated strategies or modified versions of these, evaluation still needs to be conducted. At a minimum, teachers need to know if (1) students are actually using the strategy, (2) its use has a positive effect on performance, and (3) students see the strategy as being valuable and manageable.

Include Students as Co-evaluators

As much as possible, students should be included as partners in the evaluation process. This increases their sense of ownership and provides them with a sense of how they are doing. Co-evaluation has advantages for teachers as well. It provides a practical means for reducing the teacher's load — the student shares this load by completing part of the evaluation process. Teachers stand to gain much greater insight into the effectiveness of the strategy and their instruction.

What things can students be expected to evaluate? The most obvious thing that comes to mind is their written products. For example, if a strategy is designed to help students produce more support for their arguments, use certain types of words, include specific parts, or make revisions, students can learn to make and record the necessary evaluations. While teachers will need to monitor the accuracy of students' assessments (more so at first), we have been impressed with children's interest and precision at making their own evaluations.

Students can also assist in the decision-making process during instruction. The strategy instruction model presented in this book emphasizes that individualized, initial performance criteria be established for each stage of instruction; students do not move to the next stage of instruction until they are ready to do so. For example, the criteria for completion of COLLABORATIVE PRACTICE for the "three step" essay strategy presented in Chapter 3 might include: (1) using all or nearly all of the strategy steps without prompting; (2) writing a corresponding essay with all the basic parts; and (3) developing three reasons to support the premise in the essay. After writing a paper, students can be asked to help the teacher by evaluating their success in meeting each of the criteria. If the criteria are not met, then students and teacher can conjointly decide what needs to be done next. Do they simply need more practice in applying the strategy? Does the teacher need to provide more assistance (temporarily) in using some particular aspect of the strategy? Does the teacher need to provide additional instruction? Do changes in the strategy need to be made?

In addition, students should be encouraged to evaluate their own progress during instruction. Appropriate self-questions include:

Am I ready to move to the next step?

Think back, what went right today?

Think back, have I had any problems with this?

Do I need to do anything different?

Do I need to ask the teacher or a friend for help?

By asking students to share their reflections on these and similar questions, teachers can gain valuable insight into students' progress and readiness for moving on.

Once students are effectively using a strategy, we encourage teachers to solicit recommendations and feedback concerning what they liked and did not like about the strategy and accompanying instructional procedures. Students are unlikely to use, adapt, or maintain writing strategies that they do not view as being efficient, effective, useful, or reasonable. Sample questions to ask students include:

What did you like about the strategy that you learned?

What did you not like about this strategy?

Did the strategy help you write better? Why or why not?

Will you continue to use the strategy? Why or why not?

What did you like about the procedures used to learn the strategy?

How could we change the teaching procedures to make them better?

Assess Changes in Student Writing Behavior, Attitudes, and Cognition

Do not assume that the effects of strategy instruction are limited to what students write. The writing strategies described in this book were also designed to change how students go about the process of composing, such as increasing the amount of time spent in advanced planning. In addition, we expect that students' confidence in their writing will increase, their attitudes toward composing will become more positive, and writing anxiety will decrease as they become more adept at using writing strategies to meet their goals as writers. Thus, an evaluation that concentrates only on changes in students' written products will provide a very truncated picture of strategy effectiveness.

Writing measures. Determining what should be assessed is dependent on the particular strategy being taught, the components used to teach the strategy, and the amount of time available to the teacher and students. At the most basic level, students' written products need to be assessed. In assessing students' writing, it is especially important to determine whether or not anticipated changes have actually taken place. For instance, if the strategy taught involved goal setting to increase productivity, then the number of words or pages written should be assessed. We also think that a strategy should be evaluated in terms of its impact on the quality of students' writing. We want to be sure that the effort expended in developing and mastering the strategy has had a meaningful effect.

To assess improvement in the quality of a student's writing, it is helpful for the student to keep a writing file that includes compositions written before, during, and after strategy mastery. (This constitutes one form of writing portfolios that students might keep.) The teacher and student can then collaboratively determine changes in quality. Together, they can decide on the aspects of quality that should be assessed, such as ideation, organization, originality, persuasiveness, and so forth. It is important to remember that no one factor should be overemphasized, and mechanical errors should be disregarded when considering quality of writing.

Attitudes. With regard to assessing students' attitudes toward and feelings about writing, we typically rely on conversations with students as well as observation. If a student has found writing difficult and painful, we hope to see this changed and to find that motivation and enjoyment of writing have increased. If a student has been fearful or anxious about writing, we hope to see this decrease with corresponding increases in feelings of confidence and self-efficacy. Remember, affective changes take time.

Indications of students' attitudes toward writing can be gained by the amount of writing they do away from school, spontaneous statements they make about writing assignments, and so forth. More formal measures can also be used. In Appendix C a scale for measuring attitudes toward writing is presented. We sometimes use this simple questionnaire either before or after strategy instruction as a means for starting discussion and stimulating student thinking. If desired changes in attitude are not taking place, then the components of instruction can be modified or strengthened (for example, developing new self-statements to cope with worry or anxiety) as needed.

Cognition. It is important to determine if students are using the cognitive processes they mastered during strategy instruction—did learning the strategy change their approach to writing? The most direct way of doing this is to observe what students do while they write.

Some changes in students' cognitive processes are difficult to determine through observation. Thus, open-ended questions can be used to gauge changes in students' knowledge about writing and the writing process, as well as their metastrategy knowledge (knowledge about the use, limitations, and significance of a strategy or strategies). Questions we have asked students before and after strategy instruction include:

What is good writing?

When skilled writers write, what kinds of things do they do?

Why do you think some kids have trouble writing?

What kinds of things do you do to help you plan a paper?

If you were having trouble with a writing assignment, what kinds of things would you do?

What kind of changes do you make to improve your paper?

What things do you most like to say to yourself while you write? Why?

Has writing strategy instruction helped you with anything else besides writing? (If so, how?)

Have you changed the strategy or procedures since you've learned it?

What do you see as the limitations (or strengths) of this strategy?

Since you are a collaborator in this instruction, help me think about teaching this to the next group of students. What would you do the same? Different?

Other pertinent cognitive measures include assessing students' self-efficacy about writing (self-judgments about their capabilities as writers) and changes in what they know about the writing process. For example, after learning the story grammar strategy (see Chapter Two), students' self-efficacy can be assessed by asking them to respond to statements like the following:

I can write a story that has a strong beginning.

I can write a story that tells what the main character wants to do.

I can write a story that has a strong ending.

I can write a story that I like.

I can write a story that my friends enjoy reading.

A general questionnaire for measuring students' self-efficacy for writing (tackling common writing tasks as well as executing the processes involved in effective writing) is presented in Appendix D.

Other considerations. It is important to note that factors to be assessed should be carefully reasoned out in advance; expectations about what the strategy and the corresponding instructional regime will affect should be specified, and assessments should reflect these forecasts. For example, with the "plans" strategy presented in the Chapter Three, students set specific goals. Meeting these goals was expected to result in improved writing quality. Because goal setting has a motivational function and provides information that facilitates self-evaluation, it was further anticipated that students would enjoy writing more, expend more effort, spend more time writing, and form more accurate perceptions of their writing competence. As a result, measures to assess changes in each of these areas were used when we evaluated the success of this strategy.

Remember that some changes take more time to become evident. Changes in attitude, for instance, may not occur immediately after a strategy is taught. Instead, such changes may occur only after students see more tangible payoffs, such as satisfaction with gradual improvements in their writing or better grades on assignments.

Finally, some students benefit more from a specific strategy than others. While it is often hard to predict who will benefit most from a particular strategy, we would encourage teachers to pay close attention to students' writing skills and motivation. For example, if a strategy is difficult for a student initially, then it should be modified to be more appropriate, or a more appropriate strategy developed.

Assess While Instruction is in Progress

Much classroom assessment occurs once teaching is "done." This is not a viable approach for strategy instruction. Learning to use a strategy is a developmental and ongoing process. Teachers and students should return to a strategy as students mature and are capable of using or modifying the strategy in new ways. They should also return to a strategy when new areas of content, curriculum, or experiences make it relevant. Strategy instruction should never be "once and done." Correspondingly, strategy instructional assessment is an ongoing process.

Of particular importance is the ongoing evaluation of students' progress during instruction. To help facilitate this, we have suggested that reasonable performance criteria be established for each stage of instruction (and that it is not necessary to have 100% mastery initially, since the teacher and student can return to any stage as necessary). By establishing specific criteria, both teachers and students alike have a clear conception of what needs to be accomplished and a yardstick against which to measure progress. If the criteria are not being accomplished in a timely fashion, changes in the instructional program or the goals may be called for.

We also would like to note here that criteria should not be viewed as milestones to be achieved and then forgotten. For instance, a student may satisfy an established criteria for repeating from memory the steps of the strategy during the MASTERY stage, but fail to remember these steps a few days later. Thus, mastery of specific strategies and skills will need to be periodically reassessed and, if need be, booster sessions held to further strengthen strategy and skill development.

It is also important to insure that each stage and component of the strategy intervention is carried out as intended. This is a frequently overlooked aspect of evaluation. It should be attended to, however, because in the hectic world of the classroom, it is often easy to accidentally omit or forget a particular instructional element.

Many teachers find it helpful to keep a file in which they jot down their informal observations on how things are going. This should include such things as what went well during instruction, what was problematic, who was progressing, who was having trouble, ideas for the next day, etc. Each student should keep a "writing folder" containing instructional materials such as charts, papers, and any notes they wish to make. This allows the teacher to easily and quickly survey student papers to note progress and areas still in need of work.

Assess How Students Actually Use The Strategy

Teachers should not assume that students are using the target strategy as intended. Our experience has been that over time students will often modify a strategy or how they use it. Sometimes this occurs right at the outset; for example, students might drop off a step that is deemed either too hard or irrelevant. When this happens, the strategy may need to be evaluated and reworked, or additional discussion and preskill development may be needed. As time goes on, students may further modify the strategy. Unfortunately, some modifications are not always useful or desirable. For instance, one student with whom we worked decided to drop the last step of the "SCAN" strategy (note errors) presented in Chapter Three. She was able, however, to make mechanical corrections in her writing, and needed to make this a routine part of her writing process. A brief booster session and discussion concerning the importance of both substantive and mechanical improvements resulted in her completing this step of the strategy effectively. If, however, noting and correcting mechanical errors had been an inappropriate goal for her (possible if she first needed to focus on content aspects of revision), or if the mechanical errors she was being asked to edit for were not within her capabilities, then the strategy would need to be revised.

Assessing whether or not, and how, students use a strategy also provides evidence as to whether or not the strategy mediates writing performance. If students use a strategy and their writing improves, the teacher can be more confident that the strategy and the instructional procedures were effective. On the other hand, if writing performance fails to improve, then the strategy or the strategy development procedures may be inadequate or inappropriate. Sometimes teachers have taught students strategies either similar to or no better than those they are already using, and thus little improvement is seen.

How do you monitor students' use of the strategy? The most direct means is to observe what they do as they write, ask questions, and discuss with them how things are working. Indirect evidence can sometimes be obtained by examining students' papers. In using the "SCAN" strategy, for instance, students attempt to add more reasons; their papers can be examined to see if this took place.

Assess Students' Use of the Strategy Over Time and in New Situations

A key challenge in teaching writing strategies is flexible and continued use of the strategy over time. Teachers should not assume that students will continue to use a target strategy once instructional supports are no longer in place. Nor should they assume that students can successfully adapt the strategy to new but fitting situations. It is necessary, therefore, to help students continue to develop and adapt the strategy over time.

Examples of procedures for enhancing maintenance and generalization include periodically inviting students to explain the purpose of the strategy and to reiterate the basic steps. If they cannot do this, they may not still be able to use the strategy effectively. Asking students to keep a record of each time they use a strategy or how they modify it for new tasks is another useful procedure. This technique has the additional advantage of acting as a prompt or reminder to use the strategy. Students can also be observed to see if they use the strategy when completing relevant assignments or asked if they are using the strategy. If the response is negative, find out why not. Regardless of the assessment procedures used, the goal is to determine if additional support is needed. This could include discussion of the importance of using the strategy, reminders during class to use the strategy, booster sessions, or specific instruction aimed at promoting more generalized use.

Involve Other Teachers in the Evaluation Process

When students are being taught a writing strategy that can be applied in a number of different content areas or classrooms, we encourage teachers to involve other teachers in the evaluation process. The aim is to determine if the strategy is being applied successfully in these other settings. The teachers should also be asked if the strategy is effective and appropriate for students' needs in their classes, and, if not, how it could best be modified.

One of the major advantages in involving other teachers in the evaluation process is they are often willing to help promote maintenance and generalization. They can provide reminders for students to use the strategy, help students with a particular step if they are having trouble, or suggest modifications to make the strategy more effective for the present task. A major side effect is that this involvement encourages collaboration with other teachers and can help promote generalization.

Be Reasonable

We realize that trying to implement all of these evaluation principles at once may be overwhelming. A good starting point would be to include students as co-evaluators whenever possible to assess changes in their writing performance, knowledge about writing, and feelings about writing and themselves as writers, and to monitor maintenance and generalization. Once these procedures are comfortably in place, additional evaluation processes can be undertaken.

Use Portfolio Assessment Procedures

Portfolio assessment provides a way of bringing together and conducting the many forms of assessment we have discussed in this chapter. Students can keep several different types of portfolios. As we mentioned earlier, they might keep a portfolio of their work before, during, and after mastery of a particular strategy (to evaluate instructional progress). Since strategies are not meant to be taught in isolation from each other or from the larger context of writing instruction, other forms of portfolios are also important.

There are at least three basic types of portfolios. First, students can keep a biography of their work, collecting pieces that portray the stages and development of a piece. Students can also keep another portfolio in which they collect a diverse range of works, such as stories, essays, journal entries, poems, letters, and so on. Finally, students can keep a third portfolio that facilitates and captures their reflections on their own work. To help students reflect on their own work and construct such a portfolio, teachers can ask them to act as their own informed critics and review their work over a period of time. They can be encouraged to:

Look for changes in their written papers and how they go about the process of writing.

Recognize elements that are characteristic of their writing.

Note what satisfies them and what does not.

Identify areas that require further development.

Record other things they notice about themselves as writers.

When students maintain such portfolios, both teachers and students profit. Students learn to engage in reflective self-evaluation, an important part of becoming a self-directed learner. They come to see their development as writers as a long-term activity, and to understand that development is as important as achievement. Portfolio assessment further emphasizes the students' responsibilities in terms of knowing where they are as writers and where they are going. Portfolios can help students more clearly see writing as a process, as their collections reveal the changes in their writing and their use of composing processes. Teachers also gain new insights about both assessment and teaching, and greater understanding of their students' development as writers and as learners. Portfolio assessment offers teachers a humane alternative for evaluation, one that is developmental and that helps both teachers and students use assessment as a part of the learning experience.

Portfolio assessment, however, is not always easy to do. Teachers are intimately involved in the maintenance and evaluation of student portfolios, and often have to establish the credibility of this approach with students who are not used to playing a collaborative role in assessment. Portfolio assessment requires dialogue that is at times both intimate and subjective. This can be hard for both teachers and students. We believe, however, that portfolio assessment can make a real difference in both students' development as writers and their views of themselves.

CHAPTER SEVEN

"The Trick of It"

One day the authors' little girl called out to her Mom, who was in the next room, "Mommy, what comes after 4?" Mom, always eager to grasp a "learning moment," started to explain how someone who knew how to count to 10 could find out what came after 4. The conversation went something like this:

Mom: "Oh, well that's easy honey, since you know how to count to 10. Start counting at 1 and listen. . ."

Leah (with anger, fueled by an evident need to know): "Mommy, just tell me the answer!"

Given the answer, Leah went back to the counting activity she had been involved in. A few days later, at an appropriate time, Mom modeled how she could find out what number came after 2, or 4, or 7. Leah, listening intently, got the hang of it and then said, "Oh Mommy, now I know the trick of it." A few days after that she improved on the trick of it by discovering, with a little help, that you could start at any number close to the one you needed, rather than starting all the way back at 1 every time.

To this day there are times for her, as for all of us, when she wants to "do it myself" or "find it out" for herself, times when she just wants (or needs) the answer, and times when she wants to know the "trick of it." That's what this book has been all about—helping young writers develop, when they are ready and want to know, the trick of it. Thus, teaching strategies for planning, revising, and managing the composing process helps students mature and progress as writers. In short, by helping students develop and come to own some of the "tricks of it," we help young writers master the craft.

A Part of the Process

While instruction in writing strategies and self-regulation can facilitate meaningful knowledge construction and the mastery of powerful procedures, we would like to stress that this approach is neither a panacea nor the right approach for all students at any given time. There exists no set of strategies that guarantee effective writing, nor will research produce such a set. Strategies of choice will vary with the needs of teachers and students. Further, no single intervention can affect all aspects of affect, behavior, cognition, and performance, and no single approach can address the complexity of learning and learning problems.

As the illustration above implies, developing strategies for effective writing is only a part of the process of a student's development as a writer. Such development should occur in tandem with the development of a wide spectrum of writing and language skills, ranging from automatization of mechanics and skills involved in getting language onto paper, to the use of writing as a sophisticated means of expressing, exploring, and extending thought. Writing also should be linked with reading, as both are acts of communication and meaning making.

Teachers and students engaged in the development of writing abilities over the school years face multiple, and sometimes competing, needs. For instance, they must balance the development of fluency with the development of mechanics; the advantages of free writing (which often results in the "piling up of ideas" with little thought for the reader) and the nurturing of creativity with the need for structure and audience consideration; the role of serendipity and opportunism in writing with the need for planning; the importance of free choice and the control of content and purpose for writing with the need to master multiple genres and styles; the value of composing in idiosyncratic ways with the need for form; and the development of writing as a tool for learning and enjoyment with growth in component skills. We strongly encourage implementation of the process approach to writing as a means of achieving this balance; strategy instruction embedded within the process approach then becomes a part of the teacher's repertoire.

However, it will not be sufficient for teachers to merely add a class period of process writing to their day while maintaining separate, non-integrated, isolated periods aimed at developing mechanics such as spelling and punctuation. Rather, skills should be developed within the context of students' writing and the pieces they are developing across the curriculum for multiple purposes, and should be seen as a part of effective communication and presentation.

DEMANDS ON TEACHERS

The focus of this book has been on how teachers and students come together to master self-regulated composition strategies. Although we have discussed many of the demands facing students during this process, we have not articulated the challenges and demands that teachers face as they become strategy instructors. Teaching, of course, is a demanding profession, and many of the challenges inherent in strategy instruction are no different from those teachers face routinely. For instance, considerable time is necessary for the analysis, planning, implementation, and evaluation procedures required for success. An ongoing, thoughtful understanding of students from multiple perspectives is needed, as well as the ability to integrate this understanding with teaching and learning. In addition, as good teaching has always demanded, teachers need to be enthusiasts, good listeners, accurate observers, effective problem solvers, and lifelong learners.

Depending upon a teacher's current repertoire, however, strategy instruction may add or intensify certain demands. In particular, strategy instruction calls for an interactive role on the part of the teacher; the sustenance of this role depends upon engaging students as critical collaborators in their own learning and development. This role requires that teachers be active, facilitative and supportive, as well as directive. It requires acts such as conferencing, modeling, dialoguing, sharing, and prompting. Further, it requires that teachers share with students that they too have things to learn. As teachers engage in strategy instruction they construct knowledge regarding strategies, the difficulties their students encounter in attempting to regulate strategic procedures, how to remediate misconceptions about strategies or their execution, and how to promote sustained and generalized strategic performance. In short, teachers come to understand cognitive, metacognitive, affective, behavioral, and developmental aspects of becoming self-regulated, strategic learners within a community of learners. Learning becomes a shared responsibility, and the traditional roles of both teachers and students are transformed.

A Few Tips

In addition to the complexity of strategy instruction, an additional challenge that teachers face is the absence of "rules". Rather than rules or set procedures for instruction, we have presented guidelines and metascripts in this book. While this may indeed make strategy instruction more challenging, it is also a source of great strength as it allows strategy instruction to be personalized to meet the strengths and needs of individual teachers and students.

We would like to offer, however, three tips based on our

experiences and those of teachers we have worked with over the past 10 years. These are:

1.   Small is, indeed, beautiful (and mighty oaks from tiny acorns, and so on...). If the type of strategy instruction discussed in this book is very different from teachers' current instructional approaches, we recommend a reasonable beginning. We often find that teachers are eager to try self-regulated strategy development procedures or to begin development of self-regulated learning either in the area of instruction that gives them the greatest difficulty or with students who are experiencing the most severe problems. If the processes and procedures we have described, however, are relatively new to both teacher and students, it is not fair to either party to take on too much too fast. Initial failure can make persistence difficult for both teachers and students. Thus, teachers should begin with a relatively simple strategy or self-regulation process in an area where they and their students are comfortable and where they anticipate success.

2.   If possible, it may be easier to begin strategy instruction with an existing, validated strategy (such as one of the simpler strategies presented in this book or in other books in this series), rather than attempting both to develop an effective strategy and become comfortable with the process of helping students master the strategy at the same time. Once a schema for strategy mastery is developed for both teacher and students, they can work together to develop and validate new strategies. Along the same line, it may be easier initially to follow the metascript for strategy acquisition presented in Chapter Two, later modifying and experimenting with the components of strategy instruction.

3.   If at all possible, we strongly recommend that teachers collaborate with other teachers, as well as their students, as they become strategy instructors. We have found that supportive feedback and collaborative problem solving are very helpful when teachers first try strategy instruction. The rich, personal knowledge that follows from actually teaching strategies in the classroom can then be shared with other teachers as they begin to assist in the development of strategic learning among their students.

Finally, it is important for teachers to remember that the natural development of self-regulation and strategic performance is a slow process keyed to developmental stages. The teacher is an important part of this process, as he or she acts as a model of self-regulation, strategic performance, problem solving, and coping with difficulties. Yet becoming a model of this sort is also a developmental process, one that teachers should give themselves time to experience. We too are still learning about effective strategy instruction, and would like to hear from teachers about what worked or didn't work in their classrooms and their experiences with strategy instruction. We are also interested in hearing from students and in reading pieces of their work.

Types of Content Included in Students' Essays

FUNCTIONAL CONTENT

Premise

Statements indicating one side or another of an issue.
"I think school rules are necessary."
"Other people think that school rules are not necessary."

Reasons

Explanations put forward to support or refute a premise.
"First, rules help to insure no one gets hurt."
"I disagree, if there were no rules, then nothing would get done."

Conclusion

A statement that closes up what has been written or brings everything together.
"That is why I believe rules are necessary."

Elaborations

Saying more or giving an example for a premise, reason, or conclusion.
"I think that school rules are necessary, *but only for very young children.*"
"For example, if there were no rules, no teaching would be done because the children would not pay attention."

NONFUNCTIONAL TEXT

Nonfunctional Repetition

Repeating material without any discernible rhetorical purpose.

"That is why I believe rules are necessary. *I believe school rules are necessary.*"

Nonfunctional Other

Presenting material unrelated to the argument.

"I like to write about things like this."

Note: Functional text is any text that supports the development of the argument; nonfunctional text does not.

A Scale for Scoring the Inclusion and Quality of the Parts of a Story

STUDENT'S NAME _____

TOTAL SCORE _____

DIRECTIONS: Read the story once to get a general impression, then look at the story again to score each part. For each part, circle the appropriate rating. Total the sum of the ratings and enter the score in the space above.

1. Main Character

    0 — No main character is established.

    1 — A main character is presented; however, he/she is just a name on a page. Very little information or detail about the main character is provided.

    2 — A main character is presented and described in such detail that he/she is always "real" for you.

2. Locale

    0 — No locale or place is mentioned.

    1 — Locale given, but little description offered—"the town of Atlanta".

    2 — Locale given, with more complete description offered or unusual locale is chosen — "the town of Atlanta which sets between two rivers and covered a space of three square miles".

      — "the new planet, Andromea."

3. Time

    0 — No time given.

    1 — Time given, but traditional in reference—"once upon a time"—"a long time ago."

2 — Time given, but unusual in reference or more complete description — "March 31st at 3:00 in the afternoon" — "a long time ago, before men walked on the earth."

4. Starter Event

0 — The precipitating event which causes the main character to establish a goal is not presented.

1 — The precipitating event which causes the main character to establish a goal is presented. The precipitating event can be a natural occurrence (a landslide), an internal response (loneliness), or an external action (the dragon stole the jewel).

2 — Add one point if the precipitating event is complex, unusual, or well described — "A meteor hit the mountain, and that started a landslide which hit the village. As a result the man lost everything that he owned" — "His mother left him home day after day. As a result, Johnny was lonely."

5. Goal

0 — The goal or purpose of the main character is not established.

1 — The goal or purpose of the main character is established but not clearly articulated—"Bill set off to do something."

2 — The goal or purpose of the main character is clearly articulated — "Bill decided that he would rescue his friend."

3 — Add one additional point if two or more goals are clearly articulated.

6. Action

0 — The actions that the main character initiates in order to achieve the goal are not presented.

1 — What the main character does in order to achieve the main goals is presented.

2-4   Add one point for each of the following:

A. Actions or events happen in a logical order (i.e., they are not inconsistent).

B. Ingenuity or originality are used to solve situations or

predicaments — "Bill made a laser-reflector to capture his enemy."

C. If there is more than one well-defined episode. For example, if the main character tries one action and it is unsuccessful (storms the castle but has to retreat due to boiling oil) and then tries another action (tries to sneak in through a tunnel), add one point. Similarly, if the main character goes to one place during his travels and then to another, add one point.

7. Ending

0 — No real ending, lack of conclusion, or story seems unfinished. In other words, the long-range consequences of the main character's actions are not resolved.

1 — Long range consequences of main character's actions are resolved, but the ending or conclusion is fairly common — "They lived happily ever after — Billy slew the dragon and rescued the princess."

2 — Long-range consequences of main character's actions are resolved. In addition, the conclusion or ending is unusual, or the ending contains a moral —"This is how he got the name Eagle-Arrow — It just goes to show crime doesn't pay." — "The prince was killed, and so was his horse."

8. Reaction (expressed anywhere in the story)

0 — The emotional reactions of the main character are not presented.

1 — Some emotional feelings expressed by the main character. — "The boy was happy with what he had done."

2 — Emotional feelings of the main character expressed with depth. - "I hated everyone in that black moment. I felt hot anger. Why did they have to humiliate me?"

Note: You may duplicate the instrument, if you wish to use it.

Attitudes Toward Writing Scale

1. I like to write.

1	2	3	4	5
Strongly Disagree	Disagree	Unsure	Agree	Strongly Agree

2. I would rather read than write.

1	2	3	4	5
Strongly Disagree	Disagree	Unsure	Agree	Strongly Agree

3. I do writing of my own outside of school.

1	2	3	4	5
Strongly Disagree	Disagree	Unsure	Agree	Strongly Agree

4. I avoid writing whenever I can.

1	2	3	4	5
Strongly Disagree	Disagree	Unsure	Agree	Strongly Agree

5. I would rather write than do math problems.

1	2	3	4	5
Strongly Disagree	Disagree	Unsure	Agree	Strongly Agree

6. Writing is a waste of time.

1	2	3	4	5
Strongly Disagree	Disagree	Unsure	Agree	Strongly Agree

Source: Graham, S., Schwartz, S., & MacArthur, C. (1990). *Learning disabled and normally achieving students' knowledge of writing and the composing process, attitude toward writing, and self-efficacy.* Manuscript submitted for publication.

Note: Items 2, 4, and 6 are worded in a negative direction; to make the scoring system similar on all items, change scores of 1 to 5, 2 to 4, 4 to 2, and 5 to 1. (You may duplicate the instrument, if you wish to use it.)

Writing Self-Efficacy Scale

1. When writing a paper, it is easy for me to get ideas.

1	2	3	4	5
Strongly Disagree	Disagree	Unsure	Agree	Strongly Agree

2. When writing a paper, it is hard for me to organize my ideas.

1	2	3	4	5
Strongly Disagree	Disagree	Unsure	Agree	Strongly Agree

3. When my class is asked to write a report, mine is one of the best.

1	2	3	4	5
Strongly Disagree	Disagree	Unsure	Agree	Strongly Agree

4. When writing a paper, it is easy for me to get started.

1	2	3	4	5
Strongly Disagree	Disagree	Unsure	Agree	Strongly Agree

5. When writing a paper, I find it easy to make all of the changes I need to make.

1	2	3	4	5
Strongly Disagree	Disagree	Unsure	Agree	Strongly Agree

6. When writing a paper, it is easy for me to write my ideas into good sentences.

1	2	3	4	5
Strongly Disagree	Disagree	Unsure	Agree	Strongly Agree

7. When my class is asked to write a story, mine is one of the best.

1	2	3	4	5
Strongly Disagree	Disagree	Unsure	Agree	Strongly Agree

8. When writing a paper, it is hard for me to keep the paper going.

1	2	3	4	5
Strongly Disagree	Disagree	Unsure	Agree	Strongly Agree

9. When my class is asked to write a book report, mine is one of the best.

1	2	3	4	5
Strongly Disagree	Disagree	Unsure	Agree	Strongly Agree

10. When writing a paper, it is hard for me to correct my mistakes.

1	2	3	4	5
Strongly Disagree	Disagree	Unsure	Agree	Strongly Agree

Source: Graham, S., Schwartz, S., & MacArthur, C. (1990). *Learning disabled and normally achieving students' knowledge of writing and the composing process, attitude toward writing,and self-efficacy.* Manuscript submitted for publication.

NOTE: Items 3, 7, and 9 measure efficacy in doing common writing assignments; all the rest of the items measure efficacy for carrying out specific writing processes.

NOTE: Items 2, 8, and 10 are worded in a negative direction; to make the scoring system similar on all items, change scores of 1 to 5, 2 to 4, 4 to 2, and 5 to 1.

NOTE: You may duplicate the instrument, if you wish to use it.

References

Applebee, A. (1984). Writing and Reasoning. *Review of Educational Research, 54,* 577-596.

Atwell.N. (1987). *In the middle: Reading, writing, and learning from adolescents.* Portsmith, NH: Heineman.

Barenbaum, E. (1983). Writing in the special class. *Topics in Learning and Learning Disabilities, 3,* 12-20.

Bereiter, C., & Scardamalia, M. (1982). From conversation to composition: The role of instruction in a developmental process. In R. Glaser (Ed.), *Advances in instructional psychology.* (Vol.2,pp.1-64). Hillsdale, NJ: Lawrence Erlbaum Associates

Bjorklund, D. (1990). *Children's strategies: Contemporary views of cognitive development.* Hillsdale, NJ: Lawrence Erlbaum Associates.

Bos, C. (1988). Process-oriented writing: Instructional implications for mildly handicapped students. *Exceptional Children, 54,* 521-527.

Bridge, C., & Hiebert, E. (1985). A comparison of classroom writing practices, teachers' perceptions of their writing instruction, and textbook recommendations on writing practices. *Elementary School Journal, 86,* 155-172.

Brown, A.L., & Campione, J.C. (1990). Interactive learning environments and the teaching of science and mathematics. In M. Gardner, J. Greens, F. Reif, A Schoenfeld, A. di Sessa, & E. Stage (Eds.), *Toward a scientific practice of science education* (pp. 111-139). Hillsdale, NJ: Lawrence Erlbaum Associates.

Brown, A.L., Campione, J.C., & Day, J.D. (1981). Learning to learn: On training students to learn from tests. *Educational Researcher, 10,* 14-21.

Brown, A.L., & Kane, M. (1988). Preschool children can learn to transfer: Learning to learn and learning from example. *Cognitive Psychology, 20,* 493-523.

Calfee, R. (1991). Schoolwide programs to improve literacy instruction for students at risk. In B. Means & M. Knapp (Eds.), *Teaching advance skills to educationally disadvantaged students* (pp.71-92). Washington, D.C.: U.S. Department of Education.

Calkins, L.M. (1986). *The art of teaching writing.* Portsmouth, NH: Heinemann.

Deshler, D.D., & Schumaker, J.B. (1986). Learning strategies: An instructional alternative for low-achieving adolescents. *Exceptional Children, 52,* 583-590.

Englert, C., Raphael, T., Anderson, L., Anthony, H., Stevens, D., & Fear, K. (in press). Making writing strategies and self-talk visible: Cognitive strategy instruction in writing in regular and special education classrooms. *American Educational Research Journal.*

Flower, L, & Hayes, J. (1980). The dynamics of composing: Making plans and juggling constraints. In L. Gregg & E. Steinberg (Eds.), *Cognitive processes in writing* (pp. 31-50). Hillsdale, NJ: Lawrence Erlbaum.

Glaser, R. (1991). Expertise and assessment. In M. Wittrock & E. Baker (Eds.), *Testing and cognition* (17-30). Englewoods Cliff, NJ: Prentice-Hall.

Graham, S. (1990). The role of production factors in learning disabled students' compositions. *Journal of Educational Psychology, 82,* 781-791.

Graham, S., & Harris, K.R. (1987). Improving composition skills of inefficient learners with self-instructional strategy training. *Topics in Language Disorders, 7,* 66-77.

Graham,S., & Harris,K.R. (1988). Instructional recommendations for teaching writing to exceptional students. *Exceptional Children, 54,* 506-512.

Graham, S., & Harris K.R. (1989). A components analysis of cognitive strategy instruction: Effects on learning disabled students' compositions and self-efficacy. *Journal of Educational Psychology, 81,* 353-361.

Graham, S., & Harris, K.R. (1989). Cognitive training: Implications for written language. In J. Hughes & R. Hall (Eds.) *Cognitive behavioral psychology in the schools: A comprehensive handbook* (pp. 247-279). New York: Guilford Publishing Co.

Graham, S., & Harris, K.R. (in press). Cognitive strategy instruction in written language for learning disabled students. In S. Vogel & B. Levinson (Eds.), *Educational alternatives for learning disabled students.* New York: Springer Verlag.

Graham, S., & Harris, K.R. (in press). Teaching writing strategies to students with learning disorders: Issues and recommendations. In Meltzer,L. (Ed.), *Strategy and processing deficits in learning disorders.* Austin, TX: PRO-ED.

Graham, S., & Harris, K.R. (in press). Self-instructional strategy development: Programmatic research in writing. In B. Wong (Ed.), *Intervention research with students with learning disabilities. New York: Springer-Verlag.*

Graham, S., Harris, K.R., MacArthur, C., & Schwartz, S. (1991). Writing and writing instruction with students with learning disabilities: A review of a program of research. *Learning Disability Quarterly, 14,* 89-114.

Graham, S., Harris, K.R., & Sawyer, R. (1987). Composition instruction with learning disabled students: Self-instructional strategy training. *Focus on Exceptional Children, 20,* 1-11.

Graham, S., Schwartz, S., & MacArthur, C. (1991). *Learning disabled and normally achieving students' knowledge of the writing process, attitudes toward writing, and self-efficacy.* Manuscript submitted for publication.

Graves, D.H. (1983). *Writing: Teachers and children at work.* Portsmouth, NH: Heinemann.

Hallahan, D., Lloyd, J., Kauffman, J., & Loper, A. (1983). Academic problems. In R. Morris & T. Kratochwill (Eds.), *Practice of child therapy: A textbook of methods* (pp. 113-141). New York: Pergamon Press.

Hallahan, D.P., Lloyd, J.W., Kosiewicz, M., Kauffman, J.M., & Graves, A. (1979). Self-monitoring of attention as a treatment for a learning disabled boy's off-task behavior. *Learning Disability Quarterly, 8,* 27-36.

Hallahan, D.P., Lloyd, J.W., & Stoller, L. (1982). Improving attention with self-monitoring: A manual for teachers. Charlottesville, VA: University of Virginia Learning Disabilities Research Institute.

Hallahan, D.P., & Sapona, R. (1983). Self-monitoring of attention with learning disabled children: Past research and current issues. *Journal of Learning Disabilities, 16,* 616-620.

Harris, K.R. (1982). Cognitive-behavior modification: Application with exceptional students. *Focus on Exceptional Children, 15,* 1-16.

Harris, K.R. (1985). Conceptual, methodological, and clinical issues in cognitive-behavioral assessment. *Journal of Abnormal Child Psychology, 13,* 373-390.

Harris, K. (1986). Self-monitoring of attentional behavior vs. self-monitoring of productivity: Effects on task behavior and academic response rate among learning disabled children. *Journal of Applied Behavior Analysis, 19,* 417-423.

Harris, K.R. (1986). The effects of cognitive-behavior modification on private speech and task performance during problem solving among learning disabled and normally achieving children. *Journal of Abnormal Child Psychology, 14,* 63-76.

Harris, K.R. (1989). *The role of self-efficacy in self-instructional strategy training and the development of self-regulated learning among learning disabled children.* Paper presented at the Annual Meeting of the American Educational Research Association.

Harris, K.R. (1990). Developing self-regulated learners: The role of private speech and self-instructions. *Educational Psychologist, 25,* 35-50.

Harris, K.R., & Graham, S. (1985). Improving learning disabled students' composition skills: Self-control strategy training. *Learning Disability Quarterly, 8,* 27-36.

Harris, K.R., & Graham, S (1988). Self-instructional strategy training: Improving writing skills among educationally handicapped students. *Teaching Exceptional Children, 20,* 35-37.

Harris, K.R., Graham, S., & Freeman, S. (1988). Effects of strategy training on metamemory among learning disabled students. *Exceptional Children, 54,* 332-338.

Harris, K.R., Graham, S., & Pressley, M. (in press). Cognitive behavioral approaches in reading and written language: Developing self-regulated learners. In N.N. Singh & I.L. Beale (Eds.), *Current perspectives in learning disabilities:Nature, theory, and treatment.* New York: Springer-Verlag.

Harris, K.R., McElroy, K., Hamby, R., Graham, S., & Reid, B. (1992). A comparison of self-monitoring of attention and self-monitoring of productivity: Effects on spelling study behavior and story writing. Unpublished raw data.

Harris, K.R., Preller, D., & Graham, S. (1990). Acceptability of cognitive-behavioral and behavioral interventions among teachers. *Cognitive Therapy and Research, 14,* 573-587.

Harris, K.R., & Pressley, M. (1991). The nature of cognitive strategy instruction: Interactive strategy construction. *Exceptional Children, 57,* 392-404.

Hayes, J., & Flower, L. (1986). Writing research and the writer. *American Psycholgist, 41,* 1106-1113.

Hillocks, G. (1984). What works in teaching composition: A meta analysis of experimental studies. *American Journal of Education, 93,* 133-170.

Humes, A. (1983). Research on the composing process. *Review of Educational Research, 53,* 201-216.

Kendall, P. (1989). The generalization and maintenance of behavior change: Comments, considerations, and the "no-cure" criticism. *Behavior Therapy, 20,* 357-364.

Kendall, P., & Braswell, L. (1982). On cognitive-behavioral assessment: Model, measures, and madness. In C. Speilberger & J. Butcher (Eds.), *Advances in personality assessment* (Vol. 1, pp. 35-82). Hillsdale, NJ: Erlbaum.

Licht, B. (1983). Cognitive-motivational factors that contribute to the achievement of learning-disabled children. *Journal of Learning Disabilities, 16,* 483-490.

Licht, B., Kistner, J., Ozkarogoz, T., Shapiro, S., & Clausen, L. (1985). Casual attributions of learning disabled children: Individual difference and their implications for persistence. *Journal of Educational Psychology, 77,* 208-216.

Locke, E., Shaw, K., Saari, L., & Latham, G. (1981). Goal setting and task performance: 1969-1980. *Psychological Bulletin, 90,* 125-152.

Mahoney, M. ,& Thoresen, C. (Eds.) (1974). *Self-control: power to the person.* Belmont, CA: Wadsworth.

McCormik, C., Miller, G., & Pressley, M. (Eds.). (1989). *Cognitive strategy research: From basic to educational applications.* New York: Springer-Verlag.

Meichenbaum, D. (1977). *Cognitive behavior modification: An integrative approach.* NY: Plenum Press.

Meichenbaum, D. (1983). Teaching thinking: A cognitive-behavioral approach. *Interdisciplinary voices in learning disabilities and remedial education,* (pp. 1-28). Austin, TX: Pro-Ed.

Meichenbaum, D., & Asarnow, J. (1979). Cognitive-behavioral modification and metacognitive development: Implications for the classroom. In P. Kendall & S. Hollon (Eds.), *Cognitive-behavioral interventions: Theory, research and procedures* (pp. 11-35). New York: Academic Press.

Meichenbaum, D., & Biemiller, A. (in press). In search of student expertise in the classroom: A metacognitive analysis. In M. Pressley, K.R. Harris, & J. Guthrie (Eds.), *Promoting academic competence and literacy: Cognitive research and instructional innovation.* New York: Academic Press.

Meyers, A., & Craighead, W. (Eds.). (1984). *Cognitive behavior therapy with children.* New York: Plenum Press.

O'Leary, S., & Dubey, D. (1979). Applications of self-control procedures by children: A review. *Journal of Applied Behavior Analysis, 12,* 449-465.

O'Sullivan, J., & Pressley, M. (1984). Completeness of instruction and strategy transfer. *Journal of Experimental Child Psychology, 38,* 275-288.

Palincsar, A.S. (1986). The role of dialogue in providing scaffolded instruction. *Educational Psychologist, 21,* (1 & 2), 73-98.

Pearl, R. (1985). Cognitive-behavioral interventions for increasing motivation. *Journal of Abnormal Child Psychology, 13*, 443-454.

Pressley, M., & Associates (1990). *Cognitive strategy instruction that really improves children's academic performance.* Cambridge, MA: Brookline Books.

Pressley, M., Goodchild, F., Fleet, J., Zajchowski, R., & Evans, E. (1989). The challenges of classroom strategy instruction. *Elementary School Journal, 89*, 301-342.

Pressley, M., & Harris, K.R. (1990). What is really known about cognitive strategy instruction. *Educational Leadership, 48*, 31-34.

Pressley, M., Harris, K.R., & Marks, M. (in press). But good strategy instructors are constructivists! *Educational Psychology Review.*

Pressley, M., Woloshyn, V., Lysynchuk, L., Martin, V., Wood, E., & Willoughby, T. (1990). A primer of research on cognitive strategy instruction: The important issues and how to address them. *Educational Psychology Review, 2*, 1-57.

Reeve, R., & Brown, A. (1985). Metacognition reconsidered: Implications for intervention research. *Journal of Abnormal Child Psychology, 13*, 343-356.

Reid, B., & Harris, K.R. (1992). A comparison of self-monitoring of productivity with self-monitoring of attention on LD students' on-task behavior, study behavior, and spelling achievement. Manuscript submitted for publication.

Rosenbaum, M., & Drabman, R. (1979). Self-control training in the classroom: A review and critique. *Journal of Applied Behavior Analysis, 12*, 467-485.

Sawyer, R.J., Graham, S., & Harris, K.R. (1992). Direct teaching, strategy instruction, and strategy instruction with explicit self-regulation: Effects on learning disabled students' composition skills and self-efficacy. Manuscript submitted for publication.

Scardamalia, M., & Bereiter, C. (1985). Fostering the development of self-regulation in children's knowledge processing. In S. Chipman, J. Segal, & R. Glaser (Eds.), *Thinking and Learning skills: Current research and open questions* (Vol.2, pp. 563-577). Hillsdale, NJ: Lawrence Erlbaum.

Scardamalia, M., & Bereiter, C. (1986). Written composition. In M. Wittrock (Ed.), *Handbook of research on teaching.* (3rd ed., pp. 778-803). New York: MacMillan.

Stone, I. (1978). *The origin.* New York: Doubleday.

Voth, T., & Graham, S. (1992). The effects of goal setting and strategy facilitation on the expository writing performance of junior high students with learning disabilities. Unpublished raw data.

Wallace, I., & Pear, J. (1977). Self-control techniques of famous novelists. *Journal of Applied Behavioral Analysis, 10,* 515-525.

Wittrock, M., & Baker, E. (1991). *Testing and cognition.* Englewoods Cliff, NJ: Prentice Hall.

Wolf, D. (1989). Portfolio assessment: Sampling student work. *Educational Leadership,* (April), 35-39.

Wolf, D., Bixby, J., Glenn, J., & Gardner, H. (1991). To use their minds well: Investigating new forms of student assessment. In G. Grant (ed.), *Review of Research in Education* (vol. 17, pp. 31-74). Washington, D.C.: AERA.

Zimmerman, B., & Pons, M. (1986). Development of a structured interview for assessing student use of self-regulated learning strategies. *American Educational Research Journal, 23,* 614-628.

Zimmerman, B., & Schunk, D. (1989). *Self-regulated learning and academic achievement: Theory, research, and practice.* New York: Springer-Verlag.

About the Authors

Steve Graham is an Associate Professor in the College of Education at the University of Maryland. He has held a life-long interest in writing, beginning with his early love of books. As a teacher of children with learning problems, his interest became sharper and more focused, centering on how children learn to write and how this development can be fostered. He has pursued these twin goals by examining what children know about writing, how their mastery of mechanics enhances or impedes the writing process, what strategies students use and rely on when composing, and if approaches such as strategy and self-regulation instruction, the process approach to writing, and word processing are effective in fostering children's growth and interest in writing. He was previously a member of the faculty at Purdue and Auburn Universities.

Karen R. Harris is also an Associate Professor in the College of Education at the University of Maryland. Her love of learning and children initially led her to teaching in the public schools. She has taught kindergarten and fourth grade, as well as adolescents with severe learning and emotional problems and young deaf children. Her experiences with children and schools led to a belief in the importance of integrating our knowledge of meaningful environments and of children's affect, behavior, and cognition; this belief led to the development of a strategy instruction approach referred to as self-regulated strategy development. She continues to pursue effective means for integrating affective, behavioral, cognitive, developmental, and social models in the teaching-learning process. She was previously a member of the faculty at Purdue University.

In addition to being colleagues, Karen and Steve are married and the parents of 6-year-old Leah Rachel.

Index